Ashton

·

ℋAWK
FLIES
ABOVE

·

LISA DALE NORTON

·

AWK
FLIES
ABOVE

Journey
to
the
Heart
of
the
Sandhills

·

PICADOR USA ❦ NEW YORK

Many of the names in this story have been changed to protect the privacy of my friends in Nebraska. Dick Foster asked specifically that I use his name. He and his wife, Bonnadel, and their daughter, Dixie, appear as themselves, as do Bob, Teddi, and Craig Spilinek. I have used real names for friends and family in Part One of this work.

HAWK FLIES ABOVE. Copyright © 1996 by Lisa Dale Norton. All rights reserved. Printed in the United States of America. No part of this book may be used or reproduced in any manner whatsoever without written permission except in the case of brief quotations embodied in critical articles or reviews. For information, address Picador USA, 175 Fifth Avenue, New York, N.Y. 10010.

Picador® is a U.S. registered trademark and is used by St. Martin's Press under license from Pan Books Limited.

Design by Pei Koay
Illustrations by William Hayden Norton, Jr.

Library of Congress Cataloging-in-Publication Data

Norton, Lisa.
    Hawk flies above : journey to the heart of the sand-
hills / by Lisa Norton.
        p.   cm.
    ISBN 0-312-14591-8
    1. Sandhills (Neb.)—Social life and customs.   2.
Sandhills (Neb.)—Description and travel.   3. Sandhills (Neb.)—Biography.   4. Natural history—Nebraska—Sandhills.   5. Norton, Lisa—Childhood
and youth.   I. Title.
F672.S17N67   1996
978.2'7—dc20   96-16215
                                            CIP

First Picador USA Edition: October 1996

10   9   8   7   6   5   4   3   2   1

For Gene,
who understood
that healing was patience

For Bill, Nancy, and Billy,
who made landscape home

And for the people of Ericson,
who were, simply, genuine

CONTENTS

AUTHOR'S NOTE

Several years ago in the midst of this book, I hiked in a meadow high up in the Rockies. Face lowered toward ground, deep in thought, I received a firm message: "Raise your head, *now*. Look out across the land." I did.

Soaring directly toward me, only feet above, was a Swainson's hawk. I stood dead still, arms limp at my sides, as the great hunter skimmed within inches of my scalp and landed in the grass beyond.

Hawks have long been my sentinels on Sandhills journeys—owning fenceposts, riding air currents far above my path, catching my eye at the fork in a road and leading me left rather than right.

I was christened that day in the meadow, by the wild things: Hawk Flies Above. And since then I have known I would be safe on this journey to the heart of the Sandhills.

The things we do in our twenties and thirties

are pilgrimages

to find lost pieces of our youth.

—SECOND NEBRASKA NOTEBOOK,
SUMMER 1990

PROLOGUE

By lying close in to the land, skin to sand, bone to wind, I believed I could merge with the grasses, with the hills. I believed I could become whole again. I did not know this on a conscious level. Some benevolent force guided me back to the Sandhills in the summer of 1984, some essential part of me that knew what I needed better than the logical part of my mind.

I returned to Ericson, Nebraska, in 1984 to write a story that would cap my graduate study, or so I told my academic adviser, my parents, my friends, even myself. The fact is, the return was beyond my control. I was tired, spent, like a rifle cartridge in the sand. All my energy had been propelled outward for thirteen years, since the day my mother left our home and family: thirteen years of constant forward movement. I had allowed little room for reflection. During high school, in the years after she had gone, I spent every summer traveling with youth groups or studying at out-of-state institutions. In 1974, when I graduated, I moved to Colorado for college. Two years later I was living on Cape Cod. Next the trail led to Oregon; then Texas, Arkansas, Iowa. In some places I stayed years, in others just a season; and often, after leaving, I would return again—to finish some affair of the heart, to recapture some essence linked with the landscape or to my soul. Over the course of thirteen years

I had traveled back and forth across the country so many times that I no longer knew where I was going, or why.

During that time, shortly after I earned my bachelor's degree, I was dragged off a city street in the dark of night, beaten, raped, and left for dead. For four years I tried to forget that moment; for forty-eight months I tried to bury the memory; for one thousand four hundred and sixty days I kept myself moving, doing, planning, working, so that by sheer willpower I could erase from my body and soul the insult of that violation and the rage it evoked. By the summer of 1984 I was exhausted. Still trying to piece together some understanding of my shattered family, and now trying to piece together my shattered life, I instinctively circled back to the one place on earth I could call home: Ericson, in the Sandhills of Nebraska. Here I had spent my childhood summers, often alone with my mother while my father tended his law practice in the small Nebraska farming village where I grew up.

Ericson, Nebraska: population one hundred; fading cow town, dusty, forgotten wayside resort. Bank, gas station, grocery store, and the Hungry Horse Saloon. Ericson hangs on the eastern edge of the great Sandhills region, a hypnotic expanse of rolling prairie, most of it treeless, and all of it a vast sandlot of dunes lunging up and down. The entire huge hunk of it is blanketed with a thick cover of prairie bluestem and bunchgrass. On summer afternoons light ripples through grass like a trout slipping through shallows. Hundreds of lakes fill pockets between dunes. Waterbirds, songbirds bring the air to life. There are places in this prairie where you can get so far away from anything human, you can merge with the wind, move to the cadence of birdsong.

Lake Ericson: an aging reservoir on the Cedar River, part marsh, part bass lake, wellspring of my childhood memories. The lake lies three miles south and east of the village of Ericson, down a winding gravel way called the River Road. Clapboard shacks and run-down trailers edge the north and east shores of the lake. Towering cottonwoods shade the sandy roads that connect the settlement. Here in Ericson, on the banks of the Cedar, in the waters of Lake Ericson,

I absorbed the ways of my mother, an artist, painter, storyteller. Born Nancy Sayre, my mother was constantly creating—with sunflowers and penstemon gathered from fields, with dried grasses clipped in roadside ditches, with driftwood gleaned from riverbanks, with plums picked in prairie, with oil paints and cotton cloth, with words and memories. Projects in progress defined our cabin: half-stripped or -painted furniture, oil paintings astride easels, piles of material waiting near the Singer to become curtains, pillow slips, chair cushions. My mother earned the title of wild animal doctor when I was young, and our cabin was forever filled with half-tame creatures—robins flung from nests in spring, cottontails orphaned by mowers, motherless raccoons.

Here in the Sandhills, on the shore of a forgotten prairie lake, in a beat-up old cabin called the Big Six Country Club, here resided my only remaining memories of a place filled with family; of a life before my mother left; of a landscape the dimensions of which were known, the edges of which were not sharp, a place where the colors and smells and shapes and tastes were familiar, quenching, like a great draft of water after time spent in arid land.

Here at Lake Ericson, I was safe. I was home.

And so in the summer of 1984, after thirteen years of hard running, I had gone home to the only place I remembered as home, although at the time I would not have described my return in that way. In my mind, I was Journalist-at-Large, seeking a story—but I did not understand the depth and breadth of the story. This was no punchy feature wrapped up in a few interviews and exposed rolls of film, although I first approached it that way. I rolled into Ericson, unloaded my car at the Big Six Country Club, and set out to get the story of Ericson and the Hungry Horse Saloon. I thought it would be that easy. I thought I would just write about the place, and not me.

In a very short time, though, the stories began to show themselves. As I cleaned cupboards and wiped the refrigerator with vinegar water, I saw my mother in the kitchen with a pail, bringing the place up to shape. When I gathered armloads of wild iris and stuffed every jar, pitcher, and vase, I pictured my mother arranging the buds, studying the design. In town, shopkeepers asked about her. When I walked the Cedar River, I remembered her story about the rattlesnake she had surprised sunning itself on a sandbar. At night the other stories came—dark, chaotic nightmares that haunted my days and kept me skittering around the hills, unfocused and unsure of my purpose, despite the tidy project goal I posted above my makeshift desk: Profile the community of Ericson, Nebraska, and tell the story of the Hungry Horse Saloon, its history and role in the community.

Only in the last five years have I been able to look back on those six months in the hills and interpret their meaning. In 1984, when I returned to Ericson, it was my first extended stay in the Sandhills since the days of my childhood, and that summer was the critical link in finally piecing together my life. Now I see those months as part of a larger pattern, a spinning out like the line on a fishing rod, arching, spanning space, touching down, then reeling back. During my thirteen years of roaming, I repeatedly returned to the Sandhills, reeled back by some force beyond my perception. Each time, though, I would spin away again—to Oregon, Massachusetts, Arkansas, Iowa. Then back, back to Ericson, to the hills. It was an arching, spinning, reeling time, a time when I searched for something that had slipped out of place.

On some deeper level, though, a different kind of energy was gathering force, demanding that I turn inward and reflect. This was the substance of the summer of 1984, a period of professional detachment layered against a time of personal coming to terms. While I spent the summer gathering crisp nuggets of information to write a story for my master's project, I also spent long weeks wandering through romantic involvements and "riding the Horse," as they call drinking in Ericson. Though at home, I drifted. In retrospect I find it amazing I completed the academic task, which became an extended feature story about Ericson and the Hungry Horse Saloon. The story I really needed to tell, though, the story that would join the pieces of my life into a harmonious whole, like the great centerpieces of grass and flowers and driftwood that my mother once shaped—that story had to wait until now, until I could see that all the wandering, all the questioning were part of the process of becoming whole again. My 1984 retreat to the Sandhills, to the Big Six Country Club, to Lake Ericson was the coming home I needed to reconnect myself with land—skin to sand, bone to wind—and with the truth of my life.

Six years later, in 1990, I returned again to the hills, this time a very different person. As a professor at a small college, I had earned a grant to write a book, and I headed west to infuse my blood with the Sandhills, the color of the light, the smell of alfalfa in July, the memories of home. Once again, the old spinning out and reeling back. But this time I wanted more; I wanted to discover the hills, all twenty thousand square miles. I wanted to link the Sandhills to the larger landscape called the Great Plains. I wanted to learn names of grasses, histories of cow towns, origins of rivers, the genesis of dunes. For three months I drove back roads, visited ranches, hung out in old-fashioned motels, and explored small towns, putting well over ten thousand miles on my car and discovering something I had not expected: The hills themselves needed healing. Why, I wondered, had I not seen it before?—agriculture where it didn't belong, overgrazing, lakes soiled by runoff farm chemicals, the misuse of the ancient waters of the Ogallala Aquifer. I had come full circle; the homeland that healed now needed attention.

This book, then, tells the whole journey. It is the story of a place, how I came to love it, and how I hoped to speak for it. It includes the sweet, early years full of family and home, and the return quests that opened my eyes to different, more complicated questions. This is the journey of a heart—to find completion, to tell the truth, to come home, finally, in the fullest sense of the word.

PART ONE

THE

BIG

SIX

COUNTRY

CLUB

•

My love affair with Nebraska's great Sandhills region began in the fall of 1960, the day I tripped over a baseboard in the Big Six Country Club, a run-down cabin named for three sets of married couples who built it, a rambling building with screened porches framing two sides and a central peaked roof—a shack, really, that would soon be ours. In that moment, though, I thought the place cold and uninviting. I folded my arms around me and schemed a way to leave.

We had driven from our home in Osceola, Nebraska, to Lake Ericson in Wheeler County, to look at the Big Six, which my parents wanted to buy. On earlier visits to the lake, we had stayed at my grandparents' cabin, Sandcrest, a cozy place at the southern end of the lake, easy to love with ten-foot ceilings, exposed beams, and richly shellacked pine walls. Eyelet curtains fluttered at the windows. Rag rugs covered the linoleum floor. Still, my mother and father were determined to have the Big Six Country Club, a faded hulk of paint chips and mouse nests. The place reeked of skunk; spiderwebs filled corners; dirt clouded windows; rust riddled porch screens. The roof sagged, and big brown circles like dried-up ponds stained ceiling panels.

As a family—my brother, Billy, Mom, Dad, and I—we toured

the interior, a simple task since it was only one room. The previous owners of the Big Six had built no permanent walls. Instead they had constructed a series of dividing panels on wheels that could be rolled into place to create a variety of room configurations. The panels even had doors, and it was through one of these doors that I was stepping when my toe caught the baseboard and I tumbled forward, arms extended like the wings of a young bird flying. I was embarrassed and self-conscious; my disgust was instant.

I was not alone.

There is a small framed photo that hangs today on the east porch of the Big Six, snapped the day the elders came to judge the purchase. It is of my grandmother Honey striding away from that rotting husk, head down, arms crossed firmly across her chest. Long, lazy swales of prairie grass cover the yard. A sagging wire fence barely bounds the property. Behind it all stretches a vast, washed-out Plains blue sky common to late fall or early spring.

Despite all the nay-saying—and I'm sure I registered my own distaste by exiting to the car or by some other quiet boycott—my parents saw something we did not. They bought the Big Six for twelve hundred dollars, an extravagance back then, and with that one defiant act they launched everything: the years of renovation, the weekend sojourns to Lake Ericson, and the deep attachment that can come only from long years spent wedding family and experience to place.

My family has been tangled up with Lake Ericson since the 1930s, when my grandparents, Honey and Pop, started traveling to the lake to fish and hunt with friends. Lake Ericson had been formed several years earlier by the damming of the Cedar River. Shortly thereafter the president of the First National Bank in Osceola, where my grandparents lived, began selling lots along the banks of the newly formed reservoir. In 1940 Honey and Pop spent five hundred dollars and bought their cabin, Sandcrest.

Honey and Pop are officially Catherine Hayden Norton and William Wendell Norton, known by their contemporaries as Catherine and Bill, but when my father was a little boy he began calling his Dad "Pop." One time he heard Pop call his wife Honey, and my father started using the name, too. A generation later all my friends knew my grandparents as Honey and Pop.

In the beginning, when Honey and Pop and their Osceola friends first made the full day's journey from Polk County to Wheeler County, Lake Ericson was a large puddle of water caught in treeless landscape, like a breath waiting to be expelled. A few cedars and seedling cottonwoods skirted fishing shacks that crowded the banks. From its northwest corner, where the Cedar entered the lake, to its southeast end, where the river appeared below an earthen dam, then meandered south and east through willow-lined curves and steep sandy banks, the lake stretched only two miles. At its widest it never even measured a mile. Halfway down the east side stood a dance hall, a general store, and a merry-go-round, popular entertainment in those days. The lake offered premier bass fishing when it was new, although in one of my best fish photos, Honey stands, legs spread wide, grinning at the camera, holding at waist level by the gills an impressive catfish whose tail hangs three feet to touch the ground.

The lake was conceived late in the 1800s, but several attempts to dam the Cedar were required to create the reservoir. Hopes were high for a system of irrigation canals that would stretch from the lake out into the sandy hills, bringing row-crop agriculture to the land, but each dam built between 1894 and 1916—and there were five of them—failed and was swept away by heavy rain and a rush of water down the river. Finally, in 1916, a dam was completed that lasted at least until the 1940s, when my father tells me he remembers being at Ericson and the lake was dry. His memory is unclear on the status of the dam at that time, and local history books don't mention another dam constructed in the 1940s. In any case, shortly after the 1916 dam was built, the Cedar Valley Electric Company assumed management of the lake. They strung wires and began supplying power to the county from a generator located at the dam.

By the mid-1930s about a hundred cabins had been built. The cottonwoods, elms, and ash trees were throwing some shade, and the Nuquists, Mills, Buchtas, Byers, Sniders, Dunns, Johnstons and

Petersons, all from Osceola, had cabins at the lake. It was a young reservoir coming into its prime, and it attracted young couples full of a sense of adventure. Handed-down stories paint Lake Ericson as a place of great gaiety: parties, hunting expeditions, fertile landscape for fish stories. Friends fished and hunted together, met for drinks and dinner. They chatted in their side yards, cleaned fish together, and called out to each other as they walked to their outhouses. It was not a lonely place—not a tiny reservoir clinging to the edge of a twenty-thousand-square-mile region of uncharted sand dunes, but a homey extension of the more settled farmlands of south central Nebraska.

At the time my grandparents first forged west toward Lake Ericson, there were no paved roads in that part of the state. They drove their 1934 Ford down twin sand ruts that spun across prairie. Nebraska had been a state for only sixty-some years, and the Sandhills region was the last area of the state to be embraced by settlers. Cattlemen didn't even discover the place until the late 1870s, shortly after the end of the Civil War, when the bulk of Oregon Trail traffic had already sailed west. Sodbusters avoided the region for decades more, because of tales of land like a breast gone dry. Early maps left a gaping hole north of the Platte River with the word "Desert" printed in the space, a myth perpetuated by reports from fur traders and Army scouts. And while such claims were exaggeration, they were not complete lies. Sandhills dunes are anchored now by the roots of a thick cover of prairie grass, but in drier, harsher times, when grasses die out, the dunes travel, sculpting a perpetually changing landscape of unfamiliar forms.

It's easy to see, then, how going to the lake in the 1930s was still rich with the romance of a westering adventure, made in Model A's and Buicks instead of prairie schooners, but still an exodus into wilderness. It was not unlike earlier journeys made by parents and grandparents of these second- and third-generation Nebraskans, middle-class Americans who set out from the comfort of tamed farmlands and established towns in Illinois and Indiana, heading for the beckoning western horizon with a dream of a better life. Ericson journeys may pale in the lee of those overland travels, but they were adventure still.

*   *   *

Sandcrest, Honey and Pop's cabin, was my first home in the hills, a place where we stayed summers before the Big Six Country Club rolled into our lives. It was built on a simple foundation of bricks stacked just high enough to raise the one-story frame structure off the damp ground. The main room measured about eighteen feet wide by twenty feet long. Two doors entered—one from the driveway on the east, the other from the front or the lake side on the south, just paces from the road that fronted the water. Inside the east door, and to the left, a white enamel sink with a hand pump faced the wall. Behind the door was a cupboard where food was kept, and a galley kitchen lined the back wall—a white refrigerator, a tall porcelain cupboard with glass-fitted doors, housing a mismatched pile of plates and bowls and processed-cheese jars doubling as drinking glasses. In the far corner along the west wall sat a bulky gas cooking stove.

Between the refrigerator and the porcelain cupboard, a slim doorway passed into a narrow bedroom at the back of the cabin. The room was just deep enough for a double bed. A three-drawer chest with a medicine cabinet hanging above it faced the door. There was a steamer truck, where bedding was kept when the cabin was shut down, and a tall cardboard wardrobe that smelled of mothballs.

The rest of the main room was filled with rough furniture: a plank table covered with oilcloth, pushed up against the wall between two west windows and hemmed by straight-back chairs; a wooden rocker; an oil heating stove; two rattan armchairs; a brown Naugahyde couch, and a few end tables covered with magazines. Above the dining table stretched a single shelf, upon which rested a small lamp, some books, pencils and paper, and a plaster figure of a chuck wagon cook, painted in yellow, red, and brown. He stood, knees cocked, back bent, hollering "Come and Get It!" The words were printed at the base of the fifteen-inch statue. Here also sat a stack of ashtrays—empty tuna fish cans. On the walls hung framed prints of dogs playing cards, drinking from highball glasses, and chewing on stogies. There was also one large framed image of a man, standing in a river, dressed in fishing gear and reeling in a nice-sized trout. He wore a plaid shirt, and a creel hung from his belt. His smile seemed to say that the fishing life was a good life.

Behind the front door along the west wall hung Honey and Pop's fishing rods. There were dozens of them—all shapes and designs, some with bobbers or lures still attached, others cleaned and awaiting a new season of outfitting. All around these rods were penciled comments: "Came up yesterday. Nice weather. Caught 3 bass tonight. Fish for dinner. September 1947." Or "Honey caught a 35-lb. catfish!"

Near the front door, where a group of snapshots had been thumbtacked, other snippets had been penned: "Frank and Nell were here. Had a few drinks." "Vern Hamilton stopped by." "Perry was here." There were images of grandchildren and friends—the Laases, Cornishes, Kepners, Petersons; and, of course, there were fish photos—stringers of crappies held between my uncle Jim and my father when they were in their teens; Pop grinning at the lens, grasping in front of him a twelve-inch bass; Honey dressed in slacks and a men's plaid shirt. A ball cap sits crooked on her head. She grins at the camera, holding a pole in one hand, a fish in the other.

A chair, a small table, and a roll-away bed covered with quilts and pillows nearly filled the porch. From here the view was of the deep end of Lake Ericson. You could see the dam, shaded by cottonwoods, and across water into prairie dunes where no cabins stood. A mass of vines grew over the west screen of the porch, and in summer leaves blocked the afternoon sun. Heavy green tarpaulin shades could be lowered by ropes to bring privacy to a porch doubling as a bedroom, where my grandparents, or sometimes my parents, crawled under the covers on muggy nights listening to frog song and the arrhythmic hoot of owls.

Outdoors, along the west side of Sandcrest, a Siberian elm grew right next to the cabin. Pop had never wanted to cut it down. Instead he modified the roof to accommodate the tree's growth, and as it expanded and rose so did the floor of the cabin, pitching eastward toward the back door.

Behind Sandcrest was a biffy, or outhouse, and as biffies go, Honey and Pop's was the best. There were cartoons, clipped from magazines and taped to the walls, most of which I didn't understand as a child, but which seemed primarily to deal with the business of outhouses. On the floor a nickel had been glued, a prank I found hilarious; and each year, as if forgetting, I reached down to lift it and bury it in my pocket.

Right next to the biffy and at the end of the stubby driveway leaned an old barn. Inside, Pop kept his duck boat, decoys, fishing nets, minnow buckets, tackle boxes, mosquito hats, oars, life jackets, half-full cans of paint, hammers, saws, coffee cans filled with nails, kerosene lanterns, sawhorses, ladders, and sections of the dock when it was removed in winter. Later, when such tools became important, a lawn mower was added.

The barn seemed never to have the advantages of electric light. You had to prop open the door for a shaft of brightness or carry out a flashlight to aid in your search. Sandy, rolling ground served as floor. I can still see the boat turned upside down on sawhorses, life jackets hung high on walls, and bunches of duck decoys grouped by design. Pop was the only one who knew where anything was in that barn; he was a methodical, particular man, and although I remember only snatches of him in my childhood—he died when I was twelve—I remember well how at the end of each Christmas season Pop alone dismantled the Christmas tree, packing each ornament in tissue and removing each strand of tinsel, laying it flat with the others and storing it for use the next year. When he died no one could find anything in the barn, and the adults in the family began rummaging at will, making permanent chaos of the interior. In my memory, though, it remains a place of infinite order, a room of grandfather wisdom, smelling deeply of moss, a place where anything could be found if only one were patient.

For the bulk of his career, my grandfather Pop practiced law in Osceola. For ten years he served as county judge. My mother remembers him as the peacemaker in the family, a man who quickly and efficiently stopped any domestic argument that brewed. Once, years ago, she told me she thought if Pop had lived, the problems in our family would never have come to much.

"He hated controversy in his home," she said more recently, and then breaking off, her voice falling to a whisper, she continued,

"He was a clotheshorse, always wore gray or blue suits, starched white shirts, conservative ties. He was very particular about the wave in his hair." I remember that soft wave that curved above Pop's high forehead. He wore his black hair parted on the side; the wave dipped low and deep. His eyes were set below prominent brows, and the strong Norton nose dominated his face.

"Do you remember how he could play the piano by ear?" my mother asked, and I recalled how Pop would slide onto the piano bench and jump that upright into a rag, or at the holidays elicit from the keys sweet Christmas carols that we all joined in to sing.

Pop was the son of a powerful and ambitious man, my great-grandfather J. N. Norton, a headstrong Swedish-American who defied his father's will and insisted on attending college. In 1903, at the age of twenty-five, J. N. graduated from the University of Nebraska. His father had always wanted him to return to Polk and perpetuate his farm in the New World, but J. N. did not have the knack. He planted crops, but they withered. He bought chickens, but they died. One day, imagining a different kind of life, he walked away from the farmhouse and set out on the campaign trail. "Nebraska Needs Norton" was his rallying cry, and he convinced voters in the state that indeed they did. In 1911 he was elected to the Nebraska legislature, and during his tenure he authored more motions and resolutions than any other member. He was the man who dreamed up the one-house government idea that sets Nebraska apart as the only state with a unicameral legislature. He wrote the rules for the new house, and in 1927 he traveled to Washington, D.C., as a member of Congress. Later he moved to the Department of Agriculture and designed the federal crop insurance program.

His is a long shadow cast over my family. His daughter, my great-aunt Evelyn Norton Lincoln, followed her father to D.C., attended George Washington University, and in the 1950s decided she would work for the next President of the United States. She set her eye on a young, up-and-coming senator from Massachusetts—John Fitzgerald Kennedy—and volunteered in his office. Slowly she made her way to the position of personal secretary. She remained with Kennedy for twelve years, moving operations to the Oval Office with him when he was inaugurated in 1961. Evelyn traveled everywhere with Kennedy—Paris, Berlin, Palm Beach, Hyannisport—and she rode in the motorcade in Dallas. After JFK's assassination, she spent four years organizing his papers for the Kennedy Library in Boston, then wrote two books about her experiences.

Despite these connections, Pop stayed in Nebraska, where he masterfully played his role as country lawyer, jawing with the farmers or speaking Swedish with the elders in the county, changing diction and grammar to suit the situation. Years after he had relinquished his judicial position, people in Osceola and Ericson still called him Judge. Ironically, my father told me once, all Pop really wanted to be was a basketball coach.

Early in the 1960s—after my parents purchased the Big Six Country Club—when exams and report cards signaled the close of school in spring, my mother would announce it was time to open the cabin. She perched on her stool in the kitchen in Osceola and built long lists of cleaning supplies and tasks; she packed cardboard boxes and brown paper bags with matches and batteries, toilet paper, canned corn, and pasta. She loaded laundry baskets with freshly washed sheets, curtains, and towels and carried load after load out the back sidewalk to the car waiting in the driveway, our Pontiac Bonneville station wagon. When the last suitcase, cooler of food, and sack of lemon oil, ammonia, vinegar, and Lysol was stowed, she and I slid into the front seat and began the long journey out of the flat corn and milo fields of south-central Nebraska and into the rolling, bluestem-covered dunes of the Sandhills. It was a transition so complete, my childhood of those early years seems like two lives: the school year spent in our little town of Osceola, where streets were paved and lawns mowed, where classmates were farmers' children and merchants' kids; and my summers spent in a world of sand roads, prairie pastures, marsh shallows thick with tadpoles and dragonflies, and scrappy ranch kids on horseback who spun ropes longer than they were tall.

One hundred miles: the distance from Osceola to Lake Ericson was as far as China in my mind. I measured our progress in the land. I knew the order of the small towns along the route and ticked off the population signs and directional arrows, the billboards advertising restful sleep in motels like the Rodeo, and seed-corn signs and cattle Brand Inspection notices that marked the shift from farmland to ranchland. I knew when the earth faded from black dirt to whitewashed sand that we were halfway to St. Paul, and St. Paul was halfway to the lake.

"Goin' to the lake" was a prominent phrase in our vocabulary.

"Goin' to the lake?" Honey would ask.

Or "We're goin' to the lake!" Billy and I would chime.

"I'm goin' up to the lake this weekend," my father would say, and then run through a list of lumber and supplies he would lash to the top of the car and heap in its long back compartment. He and my mother would discuss the next phase of renovation while Billy and I hung on those magical words.

"Can I go? Can I go?" we would repeat over and over, until our parents fairly threw their answer at us.

"No!"

"Your father wants to get some work done," my mother would say. And so my dad would drive off into the night alone, loading the car late after work on Friday, disappearing into the horizon west of our house long after we'd crawled into bed, and returning again late at night after we had been tucked in on Sunday.

My father has always loved projects: gardens, planting trees, and building, which seems to be his favorite. He loves to sketch out in his mind how the pieces will fit together, how the tools will transform the wood and hardware into his vision. He is a tall, lean man who looks Swedish: reddish-blond hair, deep-set blue eyes, fair skin. A strong nose and chin frame his face. By profession he is a lawyer, like his father and brother, all of whom graduated from the law school at the University of Nebraska.

When my father earned his degree, he returned to Osceola to practice law with Pop. He was a bulldog lawyer, and he seldom lost a case. His strength lay in his gift for argument and his creative use of theatrics, which enhanced his courtroom performance. In 1961, he was Governor Frank Morrison's choice for U.S. district attorney for Nebraska. His name was one of three submitted to Bobby Kennedy for that post, but my father pulled out. Years later he would tell me he thought that was the first occasion when my mother's feelings for him wavered.

Later Morrison appointed Dad to the Nebraska Power Review Board, a special agency created to regulate the electrical industry in the state. Within a year my father was chairman, a position he held for six years, all the while pushing Nebraska's power industry toward regional planning. Maneuvering and negotiating, he staged major electrical tie-ins with Colorado, South Dakota, and Iowa. He was a mover and shaker in Nebraska during those days, and he was often pictured and quoted in state newspapers.

My mother met my father at the University of Nebraska, where they were students, but it was only by chance that Nancy Sayre even ended up in Nebraska. She lived in Longmeadow, Massachusetts, with her parents, Dale and Lucille. She had attended Denison University and was in the process of transferring to Northwestern, where she had been accepted to the Medill School of Journalism. At that moment, though, her father's job took him to Lincoln, Nebraska, where he became national sales manager for Cushman Motors, and by some twist of fate my mother opted to forgo the Northwestern acceptance and applied to the University of Nebraska, to be near her parents. The year was 1949. She pledged a sorority, Kappa Kappa Gamma. My father was president of the Sigma Alpha Epsilon fraternity right across the street. Perhaps he saw my mother drive up in her black Cadillac. She was a tall, outspoken woman with a fair measure of Irish in her blood. Her auburn hair tumbled below her shoulders; fiery brown eyes sparked when she got riled, and she had great gams, as they would have said in the forties. She was known around campus as extremely bright and incorrigibly adventurous. Once she stepped onto the fire escape of the Kappa house and fired one shot from her .22 rifle—a Winchester given to her by her father, who was a nationally recognized marksman—at the street light shining in her window. One shot was all it took.

My mother remembers that on her first date with my father they went to a movie. From what I can gather, though, they didn't exactly hit it off. And yet, later, for some reason, for some collection of reasons, perhaps—all now lost to history—they began dating. My father was walking tall in the Norton shadow. He was well respected on campus, by professors and students alike; his potential looked good. He told my mother he was going to be governor. I guess that tipped the balance for her. Their wedding photos, from April 1951, show two handsome young people, happy, a little dazed, joining their lives in a ceremony of black tuxedos, cream-colored satin, and daffodils.

In the spring of 1951, when my father graduated from law school and my mother earned her B.A. in journalism, they returned to Osceola and managed the swimming pool for the summer, stock-piling money for an epic trip they had planned. It was only six years since the end of World War II, but my parents intended to bicycle Europe—a common event today, but something Americans simply did not do in the 1950s. They saved their money through the summer and then in early fall, old J. N., still alive and retired in Polk County, bought my parents' car, filling their pockets with extra cash. In August they took a bus east, headed for New York City, where they boarded a Greek liner bound for the Continent.

That six-week trip has taken on mythic proportions; the stories still pepper conversations I have with my parents. "When your mother and I were in Switzerland . . ." my father will begin, or whenever I knife peanut butter onto a slice of bread my mother will tell the story of the jar she dropped in Italy when they were penniless and hungry: "Your father was ready to kill me. . . ." In the photographs from that trip I see two plucky young people, on a great adventure—together. My mother wears a long peasant skirt and tennis shoes; her hair hangs in dark waves over her shoulders. In another, a scarf pulls her hair from her face as she asks directions of a policeman in Belgium. My father stands near the pier in Cherbourg, France, sporting a beret. In Freiburg, Germany, he poses, tall and lean, near an ornate water fountain. In Holland they straddle their bikes; children swarm my mother. They sit at a roadside table in France, talking with newly made friends.

Somewhere along the trail they sold their bikes; realizing that everyone traveling the roads was auto-stopping, as they called it— or hitchhiking—they joined the legions of Brits and Australians touring Europe. Later they noticed that seasoned travelers had silk flags attached to the back of their packs, signaling their nationality, and so in Switzerland, Bill and Nancy bought a small bottle of paint, spread out their leather jackets on the ground in the park in Bern, and painted "Nebraska" and "U.S.A." on the backs of their jackets. Those jackets still hang in the house in Osceola, leather cracked, paint peeling, chipped, but still legible.

Over many years of weekend trips to Lake Ericson, and through the efforts of both my parents, the Big Six Country Club grew into a very different kind of place. A breakfast bar appeared. Running water splashed into a sink built along the west wall. A white enamel stove and refrigerator materialized. Bedrooms with real walls and doors divided the main room. Floors gleamed. The smells of fresh paint and linseed oil replaced those of skunk and mouse. Carpets, bedspreads, curtains, couches, rocking chairs, tables, and stools all took their places.

Traditionally it was my mother's task to open the doors of this little house in spring, to air out the pent-up smell of winter, to polish mirrors, wash windows, and make lists for the next phase of remodeling. With this mission she and I set out in late May or early June—I with images of cottonwoods and sunflowers, marsh grass and nights curled in bed watching stars spin in big blue heavens; my mother, perhaps, envisioning buckets and vinegar and warm yellow afternoon wind song, chill mornings, the wren's welcoming notes.

Trips to the Big Six Country Club took on a familiar rhythm. Forty miles north of St. Paul, just beyond the Cedar River, we turned our car onto the River Road, a meandering, cottonwood-lined gravel trail that swept north and west, tracing for seven miles the flow of the Cedar. At the arrow and sign for Lake Ericson we swung the Pontiac down the sandy slope and into the region called the lake. The ping of gravel in wheel wells subsided. The road turned into a one-lane sand trail: two tire tracks paralleling a hump of grassy soil. We headed west about a half mile, past the old merry-go-round turned picnic pavilion, down the short stretch of oiled street, past the falling-down brown tar-paper shack, past the row of cedars where the artesian spring bubbled into the ditch, past the open field thick with horsetail and sunflowers, and past the iron gate at the end of the front walk of the Big Six Country Club.

The car eased over the outer edge of the sand rut trail and pitched into the driveway. I hopped out, keys in hand, worked the padlock free, and hauled the iron gate across the drive so the car could pass into the yard. Grass purred at the bottom of the car as my mother maneuvered for the back door, then cut the engine. A world of bobwhites and mourning doves filled my ears. My mother kicked aside gray elm branches that had fallen and dried on the back stoop, unlocked the outer padlock, pushed through the musty dark of the porch to the inner door separating porch from main room, unbolted it, and we were in.

A rush of activity followed: Plug in fuses, swing open front door, throw open east door, pull up shades, grab the heavy black phone and call for time, set the Seth Thomas, raise the bangboards, lower the storm windows, prime the pump, unlock the biffy, and hoist the Pirates flag.

Water flowed, the clock ticked, the refrigerator hummed, the smell of skunk rose and slipped out windows on the insistent south wind. My mother handed me an apple and told me to run along. Later I would be expected to clean my room, but for now I was sent out to explore. I imagine she put on the coffeepot and sat down with her lists.

I left immediately for Sandcrest, hurrying along the lake road in hot sand, listening to cottonwood leaves. I pulled open the front door. "Honey, I'm here."

"Oh, punkin—" she called, and dropped what she was doing. She set a plate of shortbread cookies on the coffee table by the couch, poured lemonade, pulled up the rocker, and sat down to find out about my world.

A tiny woman, perhaps five feet tall, with short curly hair forever colored a soft lemon yellow, Honey honored almost above her sense of duty the notion of fun. Her laughter bubbled up in throaty spurts, finally erupting in a raucous cackle. She laughed easily and often and happily left work for play, so when I begged for a game of Snake Eyes, she submitted and we rolled the dice for hours, laughing and rocking in our chairs.

Honey was a Hayden, English by birth, and she never let her boys forget that heritage. She grew up in a small Nebraska town called Bloomington, poised on a bluff overlooking the Republican River near the Kansas border. Her father, whom she has called Daddy all her life, ran a general store there, and she and her sister, Josephine, and her mother, Kate, and her daddy, Walter, lived what came down to me as a charmed life: a life before television, before radio, before even cars were common, when neighbors gathered on porches and friends staged outings to the river, when church was the heart of community and when the world was just a little smaller, a little easier to grasp.

On my summer visits to Sandcrest I would beg for stories, and Honey was quick to respond, digging through magazines and books, turning to a creased page and reading like a great poet, bringing stories to life as I gazed across water to wide-open prairie on the south shore of Lake Ericson.

Wagon trains streaming along the Platte, men guiding oxen with worn leather reins, whips snapping air. Women wearing huge bonnets shading pale, pinched faces from unforgiving sun, clothed in long-sleeved cotton dresses with high collars and floor-length skirts. Little girls trailing white-sailed prairie schooners. Boys. Dogs. Milk cows. Campfires built of buffalo chips, frontier songs, sod houses built from chunks of soil cut from earth, and steely-eyed pioneers, weary of the overland journey, bailing out in Nebraska Territory along the Platte, opting to stake a claim in the fertile Platte Valley, forsaking the final leg of the journey to Oregon or California. These were the characters, the settings of her favorite tales, and my sense of the Plains as a place of hardship and challenge, of the growing cities of Omaha and Lincoln, and the excitement in Nebraska during the early part of the twentieth century as the motorcar arrived, department stores and colleges opened, opera houses bustled, and the great arc of the prairie seemed within one's grasp—all rise from the stories Honey read on those lazy, carefree, sun-filled days at Sandcrest on the shore of Lake Ericson, on the eastern edge of the Sandhills, in a county named Wheeler, in the place once called Nebraska Territory.

Just imagine: creaking along in a wooden wagon, swaying and pitching through uneven ruts, traveling, at best, two to three miles per hour; the canvas cover of the prairie schooner shudders in the wind. The Missouri River is behind you by a day. Before you lie four hundred miles of treeless plains. Wind blows a constant twenty-five knots.

The oak groves of your comfortable Midwestern home are simply a memory. Out here on the shimmering prairie you come to recognize the shape of a grove of cottonwoods. You can see it for miles before you arrive—trees that stand sixty, seventy, one hundred feet tall. Water might be found there, shade and firewood. To the Plains pioneer the cottonwood tree came to mean welcome shelter, a place where others making the westward voyage would likely be found. In the shade of these trees on a late July afternoon, when the trail was choked with dust, wagon trains could circle, and in moments of silence the restless leaves would remind overland travelers of the sweet, soft lapping of waves on the shore of an eastern lake.

The cottonwood, like the quaking aspen, is a member of the poplar family, and the voice of this tree, like the rustle of running water, is the one sound I yearn for most when I remember Ericson and my childhood there. This constant whispering fused with screen doors slapping, dogs barking, and the low hum of mowers, and shaped my perception of summer.

In late June or early July the slough would be covered with heavy catkins, the pollen-bearing flowers of the tree, elongated clusters that resembled puffy cat tails. Later our window screens were covered with the cottony down of seeds blown by the wind. On a blustery day the billowy seed tufts filled the air like snow, and we could scrape a thick layer of down from the back door screen.

BILLY

My brother, Billy, lives in Manhattan. I have a home on the Oregon coast. When I look at that geographic split, I'd say we ran about as far as we could from each other and from Nebraska. It was inevitable, given the power Billy exerted over my life, and my growing need for self-definition. When we were little, Billy was a dynamic force rocketing through my days, my companion and playmate, my protector, but as we grew older, after my mother left and I had lived alone with my brother and father, I needed to escape his ways. Only recently have I been able to welcome him back into my life.

As I write, Billy is forty years old. He lives on the Upper East Side and has for over ten years worked in a high-powered advertising firm, developing interactive video graphics and advertising campaigns. He stands over six feet tall, is lanky, with a little stoop to his shoulders, has unusually long arms, lean legs, a high forehead, bushy red hair, and wild eyebrows. At heart, he is an artist.

When we were children, Billy could draw and paint, though he had no training. He built models, tore apart machines and household appliances just to see how they worked, and he had a penchant for cartoons, comics, and doodling. As a toddler he picked locks and wandered at night. As he grew older he developed the habit of talking back to his elders, disrupting classes, running wild through the neighborhood, breaking windows, ransacking abandoned houses, falling out of trees, and scaling walls to enter where "No Trespassing" signs said he shouldn't. He was what we now label hyperactive, and as a child growing up on the Ridge in Osceola in the company of his also hyperactive partner Mike Cerny, he deviled his way through the seasons. When Mike, Bill, and I are together now, we laugh about it—Mike being a master of remembrance and story—but at the time, Billy drove my parents almost to the point of sending him to military school. Me, he simply overran.

Over the years, Billy and I have repeatedly returned to the inland sea of sandy hills and the Big Six Country Club. Sometimes we have met there, but most often we have shared our Ericson adventures on the phone after returning to our separate coastal lives: "Somebody's bought the Jessup place. Did you see that shack hauled in next to uncle Jim's?" Of course, it didn't use to be that way.

In the dead of the summer, when we were kids and spent long stretches at Ericson, Billy and I were constant companions. One obsession during those years was a miniature town Billy was building and populating with tiny metal automobiles and imaginary citizens. Billy scrounged around my father's shed for scrap wood and nailed together the pieces. A small sheet of plywood, supported by a leg of lumber, made a miniature storefront like a Hollywood set. Billy painted each building to resemble some part of a small town: hardware store, grocery, church, hospital, school, gas station, bank, post office, hotel, restaurant, and houses, each with a different color of exterior paint, each with windows, curtains, and doorknobs.

Often we rode our bikes the three miles into town strictly to buy new vehicles for the Little Town. We'd wheel up to Pierce's drugstore, lower our kickstands, push open the screen door, and head straight for the bin of small metal cars. Billy was collecting one of each and several of his favorites. My main role was to assist in the selection. When satisfied, Billy paid, then burst out the door and stuffed the newly purchased toy into his pocket; we mounted our bikes and rode south out of town, a hot wind blowing in our faces. Back at the cabin Billy dragged the crate of Little Town storefronts from the shed, carried a rake to a barren spot near our grassy drive, cleared the stones, and set up the town. My responsibility was to participate in the story, to help Billy bring to life, with my belief, the Little Town, to drive cars down dusty streets scratched in sandy dirt, to imagine residents waving to neighbors, chatting about work, and living a life of consequence in that small world.

I remember the Little Town with great fondness, but looking back, I can't separate the warmness of memory from the actual moment. Did I revel in the construction as much as Billy did? Now it is hard to remember. One thing is for sure, though: The Little Town, like so many of our adventures, was initiated by Billy. I followed in his wake. I'm not sure if this was because he was a boy and I was a girl, or because he was older and I was younger, or simply because he was Billy Norton and I was his sister. My stories, my childhood dream worlds never consumed the two of us. If we shared time, it was in living and supporting Billy's ideas. Over the years I grew to resent this pattern, this assumption that my world simply was not as important as my brother's, that it did not hold the same power of future potential.

Billy was constantly in motion. I remember him as a whirlwind spinning across the landscape. In summer one of his favorite forbidden acts was to lock himself in my father's shed, cut open firecrackers, empty the powder into the cup of one of the many clamshells we had collected in Florida on vacation, then strike a match, toss it, and in the darkened interior watch the flash, spark, fizzle, then dash out into the bright afternoon to inspect the burn marks on the shell. I recall his loud hissing whisper calling me. "Come here," he'd say. "Come see this." And we'd crowd in among the seines and minnow buckets, hammers and nails, and thrill to the light show. Of course we knew we were not supposed to do this, so I was sworn to secrecy, as with most of our activities.

One of my favorite adventures, also forbidden, was executed on full-moon nights, nights when the moon seemed omnipotent, when it threw silver-white rays as bright as day over Lake Ericson. When we sensed our parents were asleep, Billy and I would sneak out of the cabin. We ran to the shed; Billy grabbed the heavy iron rake, and we set off across prairie, running fast, Billy in front, looking over his shoulder, waving the rake high in the moonlight. I pumped my legs as fast as I could, dodging cactus, trying to overtake my brother. We would shoot across the swinging bridge and hang a right onto the Point, an expanse of white sand edged by willow bushes, which jutted into the lake.

Billy began each of those nighttime escapades in a similar way. First he ordered me to gather all stray sticks, seedpods, and leaves and toss them aside. Then he raked smooth a long strip of sand. We worked until the patch was level and perfectly groomed. Billy dragged a line with the wooden handle of the rake across the middle of the cleared area. "First," he yelled, dropped the rake, and ran to the end of the strip.

I remember those nights as a field of white, silent except for our voices and the voices of frogs. Two bodies moving in the moonlight, owning the night. Around us lay a horizontal line of bushes, sheltering us from view. Flat black water rippled toward the horizon, reflecting moonlight like a darkened window. Billy backed into the willows at the edge of the lake, twisted his heels into the sand, then shot out at the line. Just as he neared it, he pushed off, tucking his legs under his body and flapping his arms like a gull taking flight. As he splatted back to earth, jets of sand spewed from the sides of his feet. He dug his heels deep to mark the distance he had flown. Then it was my turn. I recall repeatedly forming an image in my mind of the heron I watched by day. I would send my body forward, soldier of my desire, to beat my brother. Arms outstretched, mind in a dream, I became a bird, the great blue bird with a long beak and quiet ways. One night I landed flat on my face. Sand filled my mouth. Billy's laughter filled my ears. I had dreamed myself so thoroughly into avian heaven that I had forgotten time and our earthly game of Long Jump.

That round, Billy proclaimed his victory: His mark in the sand was beyond where my feet touched down, even though the impression of my face was beyond the hole where his feet had penetrated the ground. Perhaps I recall this night so vividly because I did not accept his verdict. Instead I insisted the competition was a tie: Face mark canceled out foot mark. We argued that night in the white light of the Point, far from parental governance and the regularity of day. Subtly I had been tutored to fight for my story, even though large parts of my childhood taught me to be the good girl, the passive sister. My mother's spirit, which came through when my parents argued politics, discussed issues of the day, showed me how and where to stand firm.

Oddly, I don't recall the outcome of that disagreement. Probably we kept it up until we simply got bored or dissolved into laughter; then, as on a dozen other full-moon nights, we smoothed the jumping ground, dragged the line, and took our turns. Finally we would grow tired and retrace our steps across the swinging bridge, through the cactus-studded field, and back to the shed, where we replaced the rake, tiptoed to the cabin, opened the screen door—six inches, as I recall, to the point where it squeaked—stopped. Then slowly pulled it open another ten inches, so we could slip through the gap, move stealthily to our room, and slide under the sheets.

Some nights when it rained, or we were tired from long hours in sun, or our parents stayed up late and there was no chance to escape, Billy and I climbed into our bunks, he in the upper near the window, me below in the musty smell of dew-laden dark, and he leaned over the edge of his bed, his oval face outlined by moonlight shining in our windows, and began: "Moonie Cat was out for a walk late one night . . ." I curled into a ball under my cotton sheet, ready for the next adventure of our imaginary cat, who was a troublemaker and often did things in public no well-mannered cat would do.

Billy wove the stories and I listened, giggling at the silly parts, following Moonie Cat's adventures down alleys, across dark fields, onto back porches, and through downtown streets. Moonie Cat was bold; he talked back, swore, and registered his distaste by marking his territory in classic male-cat style. Moonie Cat dreamed up dangerous adventures and executed them, slipping away into the dark when unsuspecting humans flipped on porch lights. Moonie Cat laughed in the shadows, and we laughed, rolling in our bunks until the frames banged the common wall we shared with our parents' bedroom.

"Be quiet!" they would yell. "Go to sleep!"

Then Billy would lean farther over the edge of the bunk and continue the adventures of Moonie Cat strutting through moonlit nights, saving lost kittens from horrible fates, overturning trash cans, rummaging in garages, and marking his territory wherever he went. Inevitably I laughed and our parents yelled—"Go to sleep!"—a pattern that continued until Billy's voice wandered, the lines became less frequent, and I drifted off into dreams of a rust-and-white-striped tiger cat who walked on his hind legs, sported a driving cap and cigarette, and always had a line for any situation.

Recently I told the Moonie Cat story—a solemn secret between my brother and me for nearly forty years—to my husband. He hardly blinked. "Well, of course, Billy is Moonie Cat," he said. It had never dawned on me. Never.

I can see it, though: the savvy, irreverent cat spinning out his games and tricks, always in control, always just beyond the margin of propriety. My brother reveled in such behavior. It was the same world he constructed for himself—the bad boy, the one who wouldn't be told what to do, the one who did it his way, charted his own course, expected others to follow his lead. My responsibility as his sister, as a girl, had always been to participate in his world, to give it meaning by giving it my belief, my attention, by christening it with laughter and allegiance.

I wonder what it must have meant for my brother to have my imagination confirming his stories, to have me subsumed by his world. I wonder how our shared act of imagination served to build the world he now inhabits. Only slowly have I come to see how it has shaped mine.

It took decades for me to learn that I could not depend on a man for a world in which to live, and the growth away from that belief and into some other reality was painful. For long years I felt afloat without mooring, without anchor. This dependency of mine certainly was not my brother's fault; truth be told, while I at times detested Billy's ability to overwhelm me, I adored his world. But neither was the fault really mine. It was in large part cultural. I had not been taught that there was any other way. I did not understand that I, too, needed a world, my own separate understanding of my place on this planet.

Over the years, as I worked to define and realize my vision of a life, the ties to my brother were strained. If I hover above myself and view this situation, I see the larger dynamic of men resisting a woman's separate voice. I have overcome this dynamic, partly through geographical distance, partly through sheer stubbornness and willpower, and now, today, I am able to enjoy my brother's perspective, the angle on life he shares from his New York home. I am actually able to remember and delight in memories of Billy's world, the one I shared as a child. It is with true pleasure that I summon images of his trademark behavior. In my mind's eye I see him striding the streets of Manhattan. He takes huge steps; his legs are long. His head is cocked toward the ground, in thought, but when he lifts it, a devilish glint colors his eye. His shock of red hair catches like a cap in the wind. A cigarette hangs on his lip. He has a line for any situation.

 NOTEBOOK: DRAGONFLIES

Crouched in the willow bushes along the edge of the lake, I watched the dragonflies flit from leaf to twig to dock to leaf. Dragonflies at Ericson were blue. They had bulbous heads the color of lake water on a sunny Plains day and narrow bodies, flexible and dark. Their gossamer wings moved like wind through riverside grass. Sometimes in flight, a dragonfly would coast, riding a current, but only for a moment. Then its double set of wings would flutter into action and the insect would flit out of view. I dreamed those magical creatures were relics from another age and I was some clever character, kneeling at water's edge, gathering flowers. On long afternoons I wove complete fantasies in which I was the protagonist and the busy dragonflies an integral part.

What I didn't know then is that these flitting insects were simply living out long-established rituals of competition and courtship. Males of the species spend the latter portion of their lives, the small part I observed, defending territory. Their quick movements between perches—leaf to twig to dock to leaf—are part of their patrolling of an area they have claimed. Each perch serves as a vantage point from which the dragonfly can defend his area. One seldom sees the female dragonfly. She keeps to the fields and trees surrounding a wetland, visiting the water only to mate and lay eggs.

After the territorial defense and mating dance has begun, dragonflies live only a week or so. I often found their downed hulls, as perfect as if they were still in flight, their wings a miraculous web of paper-thin membrane. Sometimes I saved the lifeless shells, imagining the dragonflies were only sleeping and that at night they would resume their busy flitting, spinning the air above my bed with the soft hum of wings.

OUR

MAGICAL

WORLD

·

I recall a summer visit with my aunt Elaine and uncle Jim at their cabin in Ericson, many years after I had grown to adulthood and moved away from Nebraska. As we talked of family and weather, future plans and memories, my aunt turned to her husband and said, "Oh, Jim, you know Lisa has always been sentimental." It was not a compliment.

For years those words stung. Sometimes when I recalled them I felt angry. My aunt had used the word "sentimental" as if it named a disease, and I was to be pitied or shunned because I was afflicted with it. That hurt, because I have always attached value to memories.

Other days I am able to interpret the word "sentimental" differently, to look at its root—"sentiment"—which rises from the Latin verb *sentire*, meaning "to feel" or "to sense," and I can believe that therein lies the essence of all art. The question, of course, is when does sentiment become sentimentality? Where does art end and maudlin remembrance begin? When does the polished image, the sacred memory, held for years in our minds and hearts, yield not personal knowledge and opportunity for growth, but rather a tight, circular path that leads only back to narrow perceptions of self? By remembering, perhaps, I can find an answer.

*   *   *

I was seven years old when my mother dreamed up a fairy garden and we built the tiny world together in the yard of the Big Six Country Club. We carried a round enamel washbowl and a shovel into the woods at the head of the slough and heaped sandy black soil into the basin. Then my mother prowled for "just the right plants," selected several short, bushy stalks, dug around their roots, and cradled the plants in the freshly turned soil. We moved our operation to the yard and collected our materials: luminescent quartz pebbles, thumb-sized slipper shells, marginellas, cones, and swirled worm shells, all scrounged on Gulf Coast beaches while visiting my uncle Jim, aunt Elaine, and cousin Miles. I scoured the ground under the Chinese elm for straight, thin twigs. My mother brought flat stones from the road. We smoothed the soil and pushed holes for plants, which my mother called "trees for the fairies." We laid paths of flat, round stones, lined walks with twigs, and arranged pebbles and slipper shells at bends in the trail for chairs and beds. This world was so different from the Little Town that Billy and I inhabited with our childhood play. Here I was in charge; here I made choices about the dreams that would dance among rocks and twigs. As I look back now on the fairy garden, it serves as a metaphor for my childhood world at the north end of Lake Ericson. It is a potent memory, fueled with mother energy, and I recall it sometimes with a lump in my throat—one of the last images of time spent alone with my mother in that sacred landscape. I could get choked up here; I could get sentimental, maudlin, but rather I choose to shelve this memory as metaphor. It helps me order my childhood world, to attach pattern and meaning to the jumble of images and emotions.

The world I call magical, the world Billy and I inhabited as children, stretched from the sandy island at the mouth of the Cedar River to the half-moon beach on the east side of Lake Ericson and down to the dam at the far south end of the lake. Mostly, though, our world was encompassed by the fields and trails around the Big

Six. My father mowed an intricate set of paths that branched out from our cabin, slicing through prairie grass that in places stood three or four feet high. One trail wound east from the Big Six across an expanse of open ground, past several cabins and trailers into my cousins' backyard. Another jogged across a small footbridge, bent south, then drilled west through an open field to the edge of the lake. A third circled around a wooded thicket of cottonwoods, cedars, ashes, and elms to the head of the slough, a narrow inlet two hundred feet from our cabin yet invisible from our windows. In the slough my father sank pilings for a dock and submerged a huge metal drum, riddled with holes and hinged with a lid, for holding minnows we seined from the river. At the steep north end, he terraced a set of steps, each backed with a piece of lumber and leveled like a plate. Then he hacked a trail along the bank through a thicket of willows over to the dock. As a child, I followed the mowed path from the Big Six, around the woods, down the steps, along the water's edge, and onto the dock, where I dipped for minnows and rested in the shade. This world of paths and resting places was for me a mirrored image of the fairy garden I had created with my mother, and as a child I found it hard to separate one from the other. I distinctly recall a moment when, having traversed the path from the Big Six to the slough, I rested on the dock, looked back at the steps and path, and experienced a shudder of delight at the clever quality of it all, so like the magical world of fairies and fancy my mother and I had designed. It was a moment of childhood recognition that the world I inhabited was known, measurable, capable of being mapped.

At the end of the slough nearest the lake there hung a swinging bridge, which linked the Point with a tract of land west of our cabin, a portion of lakefront property cut off and isolated by the slough. Upon that block of land sat one building: Cram's cabin. Cram was a doctor in Ord, thirty miles southwest of Ericson. On weekends he flew to his cabin in a helicopter and landed in the open field next to his house. From miles away we could hear the *thump-thump-thump-thump-thump-thump* of propeller chopping air, and we knew that Cram was on his way. It was Cram who built the swinging bridge.

By day that bridge served a purely functional role in our lives, but by night it beckoned like the City of Oz, complete with wizards and unexpected surprise. We gathered there, lined up, and jumped, and if enough kids gathered, we could make that bridge buck like a horse. Once Susie Blessing, Linda and Ann Melville, Joey Holmes, my cousin Miles, and Billy and I filled the bridge from bank to bank, swaying from side to side, leaning to gaze at water in the soft shimmer of evening light. Then someone began moving up and down, slowly at first, until all bodies could enter the rhythm, the exotic dance. We tuned our bodies to the pulse of the bridge, jumping higher and higher, laughing uncontrollably, as if we had been taken by spirits, as if we had been transported from ourselves.

Some nights I wandered there alone and had the bridge to myself. I stood in the exact center, curled my fingers through the fence that lined the sides, and leaned hard toward water, imagining that as on a carnival ride I could twirl above earth, suspended, safe from doom. Then I pivoted back and marched stiffly from bank to bank, walking between worlds. Slowly, I began the ritual, bending my knees to allow the planks beneath my feet to rise, then straightening my legs, bending, straightening, bending, straightening, until the boards of the bridge heaved like land in an earthquake, like a ribbon of liquid flowing without end. I latched onto handrails and jumped with every ounce of my being, rocketing self into sky, like dreams in which I could fly; starting with big bounces, as if the earth were elastic, I bounded far above homes and schools and churches, where I could see to the far edges of my life.

Dr. Cram didn't like the way we used his bridge; he threatened to close it. Parents warned children to stay away, but we couldn't. The swinging bridge was irresistible. It was like nothing else that existed in our world; it was a castle bridge spanning a moat, and Cram was King, arriving through air—as if by magic—each Friday at noon, departing again at Monday light.

Over the years the bridge fell into ruin. Someone boarded up the ends and slapped "No Trespassing" signs across the plywood.

Later the anchored stays slid into the slough, and no trace remains today. I dream often of owning Cram's cabin, though, and if I did, I would build back that bridge in a flash, and I would jump on it every evening in twilight, slapping mosquitoes and riding that wild sheet of wood, the way a cowgirl rides a pony fast and mean across prairie.

As I burrow back into these images of childhood, I know that I am seeking some lasting connection with what I lost. I am seeking home, mother, security, something reliable. All things I know I cannot have. Adult reason tells me that the past is gone; my mother has been remarried for over twenty years. My father and his wife have built a new life. The swinging bridge has rotted away. Reason has rescued me from the brink of sentimentality, and yet far back in the recesses of my mind, even as I write these words, I see an image of myself clinging as tightly to those memories as I once gripped the wires of the swinging bridge. I will not relinquish hope of reconnecting with something lost, something sacred. What succor is it, then, that rises from remembering, from the stories I tell? Slowly I come to believe that the mere telling itself is food for my soul. Story nurtures. I tell a story and I feel more whole.

On the Point, kids gathered on the westernmost edge of land to balance—teetering, dripping, glistening wet—and plummet into the channel of the river. Here was one of the few areas where children could dive into the lake, and each wanted a turn at balancing on the slippery reeds, then careening headfirst through cattails to splash into the chilled brown water.

We played there with our Lake Ericson friends Ruthie and David Gardner. Ruthie was my brother's age, David mine. At the lake the Gardners were our cohorts, even though months of icy winter snowbanks passed when I did not think of Ruthie and David, did not know of their lives. Yet when apple trees burst with bloom and school let out and my mother and I opened the Big Six Country Club, Ruthie and David were there, summer after summer. They guided us to hideouts and into prairie backcountry. We played for hours on their dock near Sandcrest, doing cannonballs into the water and gathering, after our swim, on the bank near the end of their dock to stuff mulberries into our mouths and rest in the shade.

One of my favorite activities, though, was solitary. I would swim across the channel from the Point and wade through the shallows to an island rising at the north end of the lake. The island was growing out of gravel carried downstream from a pumping operation upriver from the lake. Where the Cedar merged with Lake Ericson, the river flow slowed, the gravel sank, and land was rising, rather like the delta at the mouth of the great Mississippi. Adults understood that this operation was silting-in the lake and over the years tried a variety of measures to stop the degradation, but I loved that spit of sand. Many times each summer I pulled on my swimming suit, allowed my mother to slather back and neck with Coppertone, then set out wearing rubber thongs that flip-flopped at my feet. I left the sandals on the Point for my eventual return, then entered the world I called the Island, where I played at water's edge, stirring deep black soil from the river bottom with white sand of the Island, mixing cakes and cookies and shaping them to bake in the sun, dreaming about my life tomorrow and the next day. I explored the reeds along the river's shore, inspecting polliwogs that lazed in sun-warmed inlets and constructing mud dams to trap schools of minnows. On the treeless white expanse of sand I chased and captured tiny toads, each of which promptly peed in my hand. Cupped between palms they rode around the island as I gave a tour, announcing sights like a trained guide. Then I deposited them in a structure I had built of sand and sticks and grass. I expected them to jump out and hop away. I lay belly down in the warm sand and watched them go, their little legs pushing them back into a world of hummocky sand dunes. Hours dissolved. I sang songs and invented the future; then a voice reached my ears. Across water on the bank near Cram's cabin stood my mother, waving and calling. Words slipped away on wind: "Caa—" I waved. Her mouth opened again: "... hhhoommmme ..." I gathered my dreams and voyaged back across the channel.

*   *   *

What sustenance emerges from these stories? Why do I feel restored when I remember the island and tell of my time there? Summoning these images, spinning the story, feels like putting a Band-Aid on my heart, and once it's positioned, the story told, pain abates. Is it sentimental to recall these moments with such passion, or is the process of remembering, of committing memories to story, a conscious act of feeling, a defiant act of using sentiment to create meaning that heals?

One vivid memory comes back to me, of a summer day running home from my cousins'. A rain shower broke out. It was late in the afternoon and thunderheads had piled up in the west. As I ran down the tunnel of grass toward the Big Six, the rain simply stopped. I looked back, and a wall of water drove to the ground behind me; my cousins' cabin was in the shower. At the other end of the trail sat the Big Six in sunlight, like a ship at rest in a harbor. At the front of the cabin waved our black-and-white flag: a skull and crossbones, the symbol of pirates. Somewhere along the line my mother had created a pirate flag—one winter of long, dark nights when she spun her own dreams of spring and the opening of the Big Six Country Club. Each time we arrived it was my duty to clip the flag to the wooden pole, carry it to the base outside the fence, and send it flying, signaling to all who cared that we, the Pirate Nortons, had arrived.

When I conjure that story in my mind—that world of half-rain, the Big Six in sun, the "Pirates" flag—I feel complete; the chinks in my castle are filled. The emotions associated with the memory restore my sense of well-being in this world.

Recently I wrote in my journal: "I want my mother to come for a visit, and while she is here we will make two Pirates flags: one for Billy and one for me, and they shall fly on opposite ends of the country, linking us in spirit, to the Sandhills, to home, to our magical world."

Once I might have judged such wishes as sentimental dawdlings of a mind unable to accept reality. Of late, I think differently. I have come to believe that for me, these stories are an essential part of the healing process, part of the letting go, part of the path that leads to the genesis of a new magical world, one built from luminescent pieces of the life I lead now.

$\mathcal{N}$OTEBOOK: MOURNING DOVES

I never saw them, but I heard them: "Coo*woo*, cooo, cooo, coo."
I followed the sound to the lilac bush in the far corner of the
backyard at the Big Six, but then the sound seemed to rise from
the front yard, and I ran along the side of the cabin, leaning toward
the daylilies, listening. The cooing noise had shifted, though, and
seemed to emanate from the tall grass beyond our yard. I stood
breathless at the fence and scanned the field, but I could not find
the source of music. Everywhere I turned it slipped away, and I
began to think that the earth itself released this soft sound on wind,
that the seductive call was part of the land, like the rustle of cottonwood leaves and the rhythmic "Bob-White!" For me the
breathy "C-o-o" was woven with sun and sand and yellow light. It
was Ericson in summer.

"Doves," my mother told me, "they're mourning doves," and I wondered what their sadness was. It never occurred to me that people would hunt these melodic birds, but millions of mourning doves are killed seasonally by hunters. Is it possible that all sweet things are destined to end?

$\mathscr{L}$IVING
AT THE
END OF THE
TIME ZONE

•

Lake Ericson. Wheeler County. Nebraska's great Sandhills region. The land at the end of the time zone, the far western reaches of Central Time. The land where I learned about home, where I learned about family, where I learned about loss—and all is rolled in a blanket of warm yellow light that I associate with the apex of summer, with the sun's slow death on the plain of sandy hills, fading into dusk at ten or eleven at night. Sometimes today when I swim through water that reminds me of prairie air—flashing with sunlight, golden, fluid—I remember the hot Plains wind and the air like honey and the race of a child chasing dreams across prairie in last light of a long summer day, a girl convinced that magic ruled her life.

Imagine: one hundred miles west of Ericson, Mountain Time began, which meant that when I was spinning through ten o'clock last light in early July, people in Mullen, Hyannis, or Ogallala were closing doors and pulling down shades at nine o'clock. For a kid running through grass, warned to be home before dark, all the difference in the world lies in that one hour of light: last light.

My cousin Miles and I spun dreams during those hours. Miles

was one year younger than I, a tall, thin, sandy-haired boy with heavy glasses and a deep well of imagination. Even as a young child he acted in plays in his hometown, capturing the limelight, defining himself early as a thespian with great gifts. Often we wandered the sandy road from the Point to the picnic pavilion, sharing tales from our small-town lives and waiting for the sound of a motorcycle to burst across water. Soon our lake friend Derald Watson would round the corner. A lone headlight bounced in our direction.

Derald was older than both of us, in high school when we were still in grade school. His parents ran the only set of vacation cabins at the lake, called Watson's Cabins, of course, and Derald was one of three children who grew up at the lake during those years. He dressed in white V-neck T-shirts, jeans, and cowboy boots; his brown hair was worn in a crewcut and he had black-framed glasses. He would roll to a stop near us, cut the engine of his motorcycle, and visit. Then, like a patient older brother, he indulged each of us with a ride to the dam and back.

Sometimes Miles and I walked to the dam, slipping in and out of yellow circles cast by yard lights, conjuring our lives as great stage stars when we finally shed our youth and left behind our narrow prairie lives. At home during the school year in our rural Nebraska farm towns, we attended all the musicals that came to the movie houses. In last light at the lake we dreamed the details of our debuts—the costumes, the sets, the hush of the crowd, the laughter and applause. Slowly we worked our way around the tiny prairie lake, down to the spilling water of the dam and back through hushed twilight to our cabins, convinced by journey's end that it was only a matter of time before our dreams became our lives.

In my memory my uncle Jim and aunt Elaine did not always have a cabin at the lake. When my cousin Miles was little, they lived in Florida. Jim had escaped the broad toss of the family net for a while, living first in Washington, D.C., where he worked for the National Security Agency, and then in St. Petersburg, along the Gulf Coast, while practicing law with the Honeywell Corporation.

Somewhere along the line, though, he came back to Nebraska with his young family.

I remember Jim and Elaine in those early years as a stylish, good-looking couple. At Ericson, they spent their time dressed in swimming suits, sunning or enjoying the water. They seemed carefree, leisure oriented.

When Jim first returned to Nebraska, Pop helped him purchase a law practice in David City, thirty miles east of Osceola. Having both boys in the state must have seemed to my grandparents a fitting and proper way to order a family, but I don't think it was really what either my father or uncle dreamed. If dreams could come true in men's lives in post–World War II America, I imagine my uncle would have been a writer, my father an actor. Or is it the other way around? Instead they married and settled down to practice law, a profession they both mastered gracefully. Still, it was clear, thirty years later, when my uncle retired early, promptly sold his house, and set out to bicycle Europe, that he'd been dreaming a life of a different sort for a very long time.

Back in those sepia-toned memories of childhood, though: I thought it completely normal to go to the lake, to have my grandparents only a short walk away, cousins across the back lot, and to gather often with a family of lawyers eating steaks and hamburgers, crowding porches, telling jokes, and discussing politics. Decades passed before I realized what a secure womb I had lived in, how tight my extended family had been during those early years. That whole world disintegrated when my mother drove away into the night in a car called Thunderbird, colored like a prairie storm, drove away into night in her blue-green chariot and never returned.

Imagine a July, though, before she went. The sun rises early, stays late into night. June bugs climb window screens. Fireflies dance in night air, children's voices carry across water, a late mower cranks somewhere beyond the edge of the yard, a screen door slaps shut. In July I was the happiest child in the county. July was the month of my birth—July eighth: close enough to the solstice to make the days surrounding my birthday long and full, and close enough to the Fourth to feel as if I were cause for extravagant celebration.

On the Fourth we gathered at Jim and Elaine's cabin to watch the fireworks from their dock and porch. A group of Ericson men drove through pasture to the far side of the lake and shot rockets high to the northeast. I recall collective "ooohs" rising from around the lake when the huge golden-white bursts, like camellias and mums, broke out in the blackberry-colored sky. The fiery explosions reflected on the surface of the water, and the thundering *ka-booms* ricocheted across the lake, bouncing back from the hills beyond, so that the whole evening had the immensity of two separate shows flaring and booming in perfect counterpoint. Cars honked and raucous yells rose up and rippled across water.

Once while sitting on the dock, feet dangling in the lake, Miles and I made up a song, pilfering the then-current Sara Lee advertising jingle: "Everybody doesn't like something, but nobody doesn't like Ericson fireworks." We reveled in the goofiness of the sentence structure, and after the final explosion brightened the sky and car horns around the lake blared their appreciation, we headed for the road, weaving in and out of cars as they streamed past us, singing at the top of our lungs our newly created tune, watching the river of lights move into the starlit hills on journeys we worked hard to imagine. With the lights in our eyes and the bustle of traffic around us, we were emboldened, and inside our hearts, our dreams of stardom pumped hard and fast. This was no dusty sand road; this was our footlit stage, and we were New York bound.

Afterward we spread out on Jim and Elaine's screened porch and took turns on the crank of the ice cream machine, adding salt and ice, anticipating the treat we would consume in basket chairs in far corners of the porch as parents spun fantasies from the filament of political dreams—gubernatorial races, Senate elections, party appointments, and the Norton potential.

As children, we talked quietly, licked our spoons, and absorbed this way of life deep into marrow—a way of family, of togetherness. Our lives, we knew in the trusting, simple way that children know such things, were dependable, safe, destined for greatness. I could never have understood the rumbling in my mother's heart, the questions in my father's mind.

$\mathscr{N}$OTEBOOK: CEDARS

Like great woolly bison that once covered the prairie, they too define this landscape. At dusk just smudges of darkness against the horizon—yet I know what they are; I could pick them out at a fast run in a speeding car; I could name them in the dark. Even when night falls so tightly it closes the cap on all else, their irregular shapes call to me, speaking the story of known prairie. *Cedre, cedrus, kedros.* Tough, pungent, persistent relics of forests long forgotten beneath the skin of earth. Cedars, as we called them. Junipers, as they are known in states farther west.

Scraggly, somewhat scruffy in Nebraska, the eastern red cedar, or eastern juniper, as it is also known, is a close cousin of the Rocky Mountain juniper, which grows in the far western reaches of the state. Somewhere in the Sandhills these two junipers mingle, their differences becoming indistinguishable to the average eye. Even early explorers keeping journals filled with observations of the natural world could not differentiate the cedars on the flanks of the Rockies from those on the Plains farther east.

In the central hills they grow from ten to twenty feet high, bushy, spreading trees. I brush a branch as I pass, and the prickle of stubby growth conjures generations of cedar stories; the pitchy smell of leaves crushed between fingers is a seasons-old sign of home. I know the line of windbreak cedars just west of the Big Six Country Club like I know my house in the dark of night, the way I know the laugh of an old friend, the voice of a distant lover. I know these trees like I know the steady beat of my pulse, deep in veins, prodding me forward into the light of day.

Into the

Black Night

One spring day my mother and I drove west out of Osceola toward the Sandhills and Ericson. It was late afternoon when we loaded the green Bomb, our 1958 Pontiac. My mother had indulged me and let me stay late in town to attend Beth Fjell's birthday party. As we crossed the railroad tracks and rolled around the big curve past the grain elevators, and the horizon opened wide, my mother's forehead wrinkled in a frown. Storm clouds were building on the horizon.

"Turn on the radio," she said, and I twirled the bulky knob, stopping when she commanded. We listened through static to the weather report; then she directed me to tune again to find another. Within miles, rain blocked out the light; we were surrounded by tornadoes. They were touching down to the east of us, the radio crackled—and, by the names of towns in the warnings, to the west of us, too.

When we were halfway to Ericson, north of St. Paul, flashing lights appeared through the rain and gray. A policeman in a yellow slicker slowed traffic from the middle of the road. My mother rolled down her window; a tornado had come through a short half hour before.

"Hit the farmhouse there on the left side of the road." He

pointed. "Flipped across and smashed those outbuildings down there." We peered through the gray and wind.

"Then back across the highway to that house up there. Took the roof."

Twisted metal and unrecognizable chunks of farm equipment had been dropped like toys across fields and on the highway. Traffic was slowed to a crawl to dodge the monstrous hunks of metal looming in the road.

"Be careful," he said. "There's a twister bouncing all over Greeley County."

Greeley County stretched for forty miles ahead of us. My mother, a focused and straight-thinking plainswoman, was shaken. My child's intuition told me that, but oddly, I was not scared. What harm could come to me? We drove in silence, she hunched up close to the wheel, squinting through the windshield, and I with my back straight, sitting on the edge of the big rolled seat, trying to manipulate the radio knob like a professional, all the while feeling as if I were in the middle of an exciting TV show. Soon the script would write us out of danger, and in fact we did drive out of the thunderstorms, turn onto the River Road north of Greeley, and bomb down the road toward Ericson and the Big Six. We arrived safely, confirming my feelings.

During the years I was growing up in Osceola and Ericson, there was a storm building in my family. Some might have called it a squall, and over time I grew complacent about its existence. My mother wanted to leave Osceola, Nebraska; she wanted broader horizons. My father wanted to stay—perhaps not consciously, but the choices he made implied he preferred life in his hometown. Innocent beginnings, like early afternoon clouds before thunderheads grow. Unlike storms on the plains, though, which announce themselves from miles away, these squalls were a different kind of cloud, a formation that I did not understand, and the effects crossed into my life rapidly and violently, like a tornado racing up a prairie dune hidden from view.

Looking back, I don't even recall the last playful summer. Perhaps I took my friend Terri Howe to the lake with me. Perhaps I went alone with my mother and spent quiet days listening to birds and wind. Perhaps we traveled as a family and hiked with fishing poles to the sand pit west of the dump, across barbed wire, through knotted pasture, around the prairie dog town.

I do not know.

One day it simply dawned on me that something had changed in my family; some part was functioning at a different level, out of sync with the familiar rhythm. My mother had taken a job as editor at a newspaper. She was busy, preoccupied with work. That was new, but we adjusted. My father was practicing law, chairing the Power Review Board, flying around the country on business. Politicians in the state were pushing his name for the Democratic ticket for governor. The first political fund-raiser had been held in the Cornhusker Hotel in Lincoln. Was that the essential difference I sensed, politics? Why did my parents bicker so much? Why was my mother impatient with me?

In the months before my mother left our home forever—in 1970, I think—she was absent several times, often for weeks. Perhaps she was testing her independence. I never knew where she went, why she was gone, or when she would return. There were no explanations; we never spoke of it in our family. It was the foremost thing in our minds, and the last thing we would discuss, some kind of choking silence having afflicted us all. We should have wept in each other's arms, and yet we did not. We just stumbled forward, silent, angry, and hurt.

During my mother's absences, I automatically stepped in and cooked and cleaned, tried to keep up the house and shopping. It was tacitly assumed that I would do this; I was the only woman in the house. I made dinners for my brother, and when my father was out of town I turned down his bedsheets before I went to sleep at night.

Once while my mother was gone, I was standing at the kitchen counter, drying dishes that were still wet as I took them from the dishwasher, and putting them away. I heard the back door open; I looked up, and in walked my mother with my father. She wore a navy blue coat dress; a cross-shaped necklace of opals hung at her neck. Her red lipstick was perfect; her white, straight teeth smiled; her brown eyes looked directly into mine. My father, behind her, his suit jacket draped over his arm, walked confidently, smiling, nodding. I should have dropped to my knees at her feet and wept, hung on the hem of her exquisitely tailored dress and recited my love, but instead I stood dumbstruck, frozen—arms, hands, head, mind deadened as if Novocaine filled my veins. I turned back to the dishes, mannequinlike, unable to speak.

A hundred thousand times over the years since then I have wondered whether, if I had said, "Oh, Mom, I'm so glad you're home, I love you," she would have stayed, the next few months would have unfolded differently, somehow fate would have kept her there in Osceola, in Ericson, in the Big Six Country Club, in my life.

But that was not the script we had been handed, and after a few months—perhaps a year—of conferences with my uncle, late-night drives to Lincoln, overnights in the Cornhusker Hotel, loud talks behind closed doors, and cold dinners of fish sticks and canned peas, I was called downstairs. There in the family room sat one of my least favorite people in the world: the Methodist minister, a man with a short temper and a hook at the end of his left arm. I had never cared for him, and now he was in my family room, and my mother was pacing, waiting for Billy to come downstairs, waiting for us to sit on the couch, waiting for us to listen to the joint speech—something about "Your mother is going now; it is the best thing; God will watch over you"; blah-blah-blah-blah-blah. The words raced into a buzz like bees in my head, and all I could do was watch the scene unfold: my mother leaning on the stool she had carried from the kitchen, looking down at us, silhouetted against the fireplace—the fireplace she and my father had designed, with the epic beam we had hauled as a family from the old Indian school in Genoa and beaten with chains and hammers in the driveway to make it look old, weathered—the minister sitting beside us on the couch patting my leg with his hook, me trying to keep my face impassive, to fight back tears wanting to burst from my eyes, and Billy beside me, but a million miles away. Across what seemed a vast chasm, growing wider as I watched, sat my mother, her face wrenched into a shape I did not recognize; her all-familiar face had gone bad on me, that beloved head circled with close-cropped auburn hair, brows like tepees, chocolate eyes, exotic lips, always painted, lips that had for thirteen years led me through a wondrous world with stories and laughter, those red lips now twisted, gone thin. She wore a cream-colored turtleneck, brown slacks, a suede camel-colored jacket. She was elegant, distant, forever beautiful, untouchable in my mind.

And then the buzzing stopped, and as in some slow-motion movie sequence, my mother stood, carried the stool—her stool, the one I always saw her perched on when I came home from school—back to its place by the bar dividing family room from kitchen, turned, paused, lifted those lips, blew us a kiss, and turned for the door.

Billy and I were left with Reverend Odgers and his hook, sitting side by side on the couch, not touching, a huge canyon having rumbled into the space between us. Somewhere in my memory I see the minister rise and motion with his hand and his hook. His mouth moves and he is speaking, but I do not hear—the rush of water in my ears, like ocean, like a flood, like waves pounding, like my head will break. Then he is gone, and my father is there, all blustery, telling us to get our pajamas and toothbrushes.

"We are leaving," he says.

I wonder about school the next day. I will miss my classes.

We are bundled into the car. We drive off into black night, fast and furious, without words. Scenery I know well flicks by outside the window, scenery now unfamiliar, alien. Billy sits on the other side of the backseat, leans against the door. His head rests on the window. My father's shoulders and head in front of me are outlined by the aura of the headlights leading our car into a black cloud, away from my home, into some world I do not recognize.

We drive to Lincoln, on a road I have traveled hundreds of times, and yet I do not even comprehend the journey. We arrive at the Cornhusker Hotel in Lincoln, check into rooms, close the doors, and turn out the lights.

*   *   *

A place once magical in my mind, far to the west, nestled in rolling dunes, carved with paths in chest-deep grass, a place imbued with mother and father spirit, a place ripe with childhood dreams scuttled outright into the shadows that night, like a crab fleeing the tide. Ericson. The Big Six Country Club. The Sandhills of Nebraska Territory, the defining landscape of my youth, vaporized that night as if it had been bombed from the geography of the state. And I began a long period of functioning half alive, like an acorn of myself, buried somewhere deep inside, awaiting spring, moving unaware through days—buying groceries, folding sheets, polishing tables, writing exams. My life after that night blurs into a collage of half images, broken stories, all without beginnings or endings.

So began the long years of spinning out and reeling back—travels to Washington, D.C.; a school year in Osceola; tours with singing groups; a school year in Osceola; a summer studying at Northwestern; a school year in Osceola. Around and around my life spun, with me, Lisa, somewhere in the center, watching it whirl, yet unsure of who "me" even was. And nowhere in those years do I remember the lake, the Pirates flag, the long draw of summer poised on the night horizon.

Thirteen years later, in 1984, my adviser at the journalism school of the University of Iowa told me of a video he had seen on educational TV about the Nebraska Sandhills and a place called Ericson and a bar called the Hungry Horse Saloon. I tracked down a copy of the video and watched it. I could write this story, I thought. Not this very story, but a different one—my story—about Ericson, about the lake, about . . . well, I didn't exactly know. I just knew I had a story, so I proposed a creative project to complete my master's degree that included a piece of writing about Ericson and the Hungry Horse Saloon. It was approved. I sublet my apartment, stored my bed, packed my books, and boxed my winter clothes.

As I look back, it does not seem at all surprising that I chose Ericson, or that Ericson chose me, but I was so out of touch with those early days—thirteen years of constant movement having drowned the details—that it did not even seem significant to me that I had dreamed up a graduate project about Ericson that should serve as a rite of passage. I lit out from Iowa City with set-jawed determination to get the story. Plain and simple. Journalist at work. I did not perceive the depth of the search upon which I was embarking as I drove west out of Johnson County and into familiar yet foreign landscape beyond the Missouri.

*N*OTEBOOK: SAND ROSES

I walked far out into prairie once, simply looked out the window of the Big Six Country Club, gazed as far as I could see into rolling dunes, and said, "I think I'll walk there." And I did—just threw on a jacket over my shirt and set off in a straight line, walking through ditches and climbing fences. When I arrived at the hill I thought was the one I had seen from the cabin, roses hugged the prairie dune. Close to earth, so low I had to get down on my knees to know them. In summer the blossoms are delicate and pink, like youth unspent. Five petals each, a yellow center. Simple beauty. But now the blooms had passed, and tucked among the spiny stems were rosehips, the fruit of this hearty plant. I pinched the round seedpods from the stems and stood, surveying the expanse of prairie that rumbled away in every direction, heaving and flowing to the limits of my sight. I popped into my mouth a smooth, round hip, rolled it with my tongue, and split the flesh with teeth. A taste so bitter, so astringent, so taut exploded, and I had to bend and spit onto the ground the seeds and hull and flesh. On the way back through prairie I stopped at a horse tank and cupped water to my mouth, washing away the taste but not erasing the memory.

•

P ART TWO

•

CONJURING

I come to the writing of this story slowly and with much resistance. The reasons why are mixed up, complex and labyrinthine when I try to find my way through them, but, most simply: I do not remember the summer of 1984. To evoke the details I have to read old letters, journal entries, and notes from my research project; I have to look at photos made during that time. By conjuring, pieces have come, reluctantly, but they are not at all like the rapid, distinct images I have of my childhood or of events in the last six years in my life. Why? It is simple. I was drinking then.

When I arrived in Ericson and realized the landscape was full of my stories, I felt threatened, although at the time I could not have articulated this reality. I was conscious very early on, though, that this was not going to be a simple journalistic assignment of cataloguing a bunch of facts, snapping a few pictures, and taking down some quotes. There was a much larger story embedded in this landscape, and while it seduced me with its familiarity, it also scared me right down to my shoes; it meant looking at my life, an endeavor I was not yet ready to embark upon. Consequently, I took to dealing with the depth of the emotions evoked by this all-too-familiar landscape in an increasingly characteristic fashion: avoidance. Here in the hills that was not hard to do. The Hungry Horse Saloon and a dozen other drinking establishments were happy to oblige.

Why was I drinking in the first place? It is a long tale of years of sinking into a haze, leaving behind the bright Lisa of my childhood, washing her with substances that would blunt the pain that began when my mother left. It ended in 1988, when I decided I wanted a different life; I wanted to be clear; I wanted to know myself; I wanted to claim my story.

In between were almost twenty years of running from myself. The woman who I was abused substances—food, pot, beer—to deaden her senses. The woman who I was kept moving physically: During the first years after my mother left our home, while I was still in high school, I traveled every summer—to D.C., Chicago, Britain. During those years I used food and then diet pills and always pot to regulate my world. In the eight years between high school and graduate school I escalated my wandering, living in Denver; in Hyannis, South Dennis, and Eastham on Cape Cod; in seven different apartments in Portland, Oregon; one house in Lincoln, Nebraska; two homes in Fayetteville, Arkansas; and the YMCA in El Paso, Texas.

Year after year, I loaded into the back of my car a box of books, writing paper, a typewriter, a suitcase of clothing, a stereo, records, and a box of pots and pans, and set off in some direction—Cape Cod in the summer of 1976, after two years of college in Colorado; Oregon in late summer 1977, to a new college; back to the Cape in the summer of 1978, to visit an old love; then back again to Oregon. I became an expert at wedging each item into the rear compartment of my car. I learned the restaurants and motels along America's byways and returned annually for hotcakes in Burley, Idaho, for lemon meringue pie outside Des Moines, for hand-cut French fries in Torrington, Wyoming, feeling always invigorated by my "worldliness" but never stable or happy.

The world I had known as a child was gone, and everywhere I traveled I looked for a replacement. At the time, I could not have named the driving force behind my wandering. If I thought I was doing anything, I suppose, it was the act of witnessing, the active effort of storing emotions and experiences for the stories I would someday write. I was apprenticing in the field of emotion, learning the nuances of sadness, depression, joy, and loss. I was a tabula rasa, allowing the world to etch its patterns into me. Always, though, the longing existed for simple things: a house—no more apartments—with a yard and a clothesline where I would hang sheets until they smelled of wind and sun. I dreamed of having a dog, of a couch in my living room, of a Christmas tree. My wanderings instead garnered me self-reliance, a refined sense of spontaneity, a knowledge of the country, and an incredible knack for holding my liquor. I admired my ability to outdrink my friends; tequila and beer were favorites, and of course everyone I knew during those years smoked pot. I developed an intense style of life—work hard, play hard—always pushing my achievements to the extreme: the most beer, the best English paper, the saltiest margaritas, the loudest laugh.

On and on I swirled, from dorm rooms to friends' houses, to new apartments, to motel rooms along roads between Oregon and the Midwest. I dropped in on old classmates in Denver; I visited friends along I-80; I stopped at my mother's house, my father's house; I visited Honey; but always I kept moving. Equating growth with movement, I thought I improved my grasp on life by covering as much territory as possible. What I missed, of course, was the inner landscape, the territory of soul; and the emptiness that multiplied viruslike in its absence haunted me in ways I could not control: an anger that preyed on friends and loved ones; an impatience with self; an exacting perfectionism that made every endeavor insufficient. I looked to others for what I could not find in myself—love, a sense of belonging.

In the fall of 1980, five months after earning my B.A. and two years before stumbling off to graduate school and another round of coast-to-coast wandering, on a journey from El Paso to Miami to visit an old friend from Cape Cod who lived in a sailboat on Biscayne Bay, I was jumped by a man with shiny eyes, a man who threw me to the ground as I ran, a scream shooting from my lips, a man who wrapped his hands around my throat and squeezed until

I could not scream, until I could not breathe, until blood raced in my temples and my mind gripped and pounded the words *You are going to die.*

At that moment I made a decision. I chose to live. "Please," I choked. "I can't breathe."

The man released the pressure on my windpipe, and then he raped me—in the mud, in a dark alley, in a city far from home.

The choice to live would mean a retreat into the misty recesses of my being, into a spiraling depression, into a long, wrenching process of reevaluating each element of my universe—the concept of trust, the existence of God, the value of flowers: parts of my life I thought I had settled but that now demanded reassessment. I had to choose, consciously, the answers that would become part of the new world I was forced to construct from the foundation up, incrementally, piece by painfully exacted piece.

Four years later, when I came to be living in the Sandhills, I was feeling a little crazy, very sad, and extremely tired, and I was drinking. I believed that if I drank I could keep the stories and questions from rising in my mind, but I couldn't. It took four more years and many more moves before something inside me surfaced and said, *Stop.* I listened. Maybe because I was exhausted and soul sick. Maybe because I had a friend who believed in me and helped me to believe, too. Maybe because some greater force entered me and resurrected a part of who I had been, long ago, in fields of prairie grass, and I got a whiff of that girl. Or maybe because one day, hiking in the Columbia River Gorge outside Portland, during a time when I had been working as a journalist writing other people's stories, I had a vision. I remember it in a theatrical sort of way: I was wearing a long black cape, running nimbly along the narrow, wooded trail—of course I was not wearing a cape. I was wearing jeans and hiking boots. Still, in my mind I see myself turning to myself, there on the damp, green, moss-enshrouded trail, swirling the cape around my, legs and saying, *Your life is infinitely more interesting; write your stories.*

Soon thereafter, and I do not remember exactly how and when,

I quit drinking and began the long process of inspecting the frag-
ments of my life, carefully and with reverence piecing them into
some sort of recognizable form, working them the way a skilled
conservator works a shattered museum vase, painstakingly fitting
the pieces back into some known shape. Beyond the protective
glass and below the yellow light, there are pieces missing, though.
The vase is pocked with holes.

And so it is with my life and the summer of 1984.

$\mathscr{N}$OTEBOOK: HORSETAIL

When I was a child at Ericson, each summer I hunted the thin, green jointed stalks of the horsetail plant, one of my favorites in the hills. I plucked a single stem and popped it apart at each joint until the plant lay in my hand, a pile of straight green tubes. Then I quickly pieced the stem back together again, waving my restored stalk like a banner.

Unlike many of the grasses, sedges, and forbs that grow in the Sandhills, horsetail is native. The spindly, hollow stems grow as tall as three feet. Rough ridges run lengthwise up the stalks. My mother told me once that Native Americans living near these hills had used the plant to scour objects they needed to clean. Later I learned horsetail is also called scouring rush. What fascinated me most about this plant, though, was its clever design: Pop it apart at the joints and it lies in pieces, no longer whole. Yet a series of swift movements can rejoin those pieces, create a whole from parts, order from devastation.

ONE-HORSE

TOWN

When I entered the hills in the summer of 1984, it was a gray, hazy day in early June, the kind of day that can blanket Nebraska in spring before the winds of summer blow in from the southwest and lock each afternoon in a high-domed world of blue sky and rippling grass. I rolled into Lake Ericson via the River Road and approached the Big Six as I had countless times with my mother, or in the Bonneville station wagon with my father at the wheel: up the sandy trail past the row of cabins built like a storefront, around the ancient merry-go-round-turned-picnic-pavilion, across the short stretch of oiled street, along the row of cedars that sheltered the artesian spring, and into the open fields dotted with shacks and trailers. The grass in the yard of the Big Six was knee high. I unlocked the gate and drove to the back stoop. Prairie grass swished at the bottom of the car and wrapped its wheels.

Inside, the Big Six was thick with the smell of mouse and skunk. A layer of dust covered everything. I carried in boxes of books, suitcases, bags of food and cleaning supplies, and began in the age-old way: opening doors and raising windows to beckon the tentative spring. Curtains came down; dust cloths polished wooden surfaces. I ran the vacuum, cleaned the stove, scrubbed the refrigerator; it was a ritualistic cleansing, the significance of which I could not have seen.

Day two: I wandered the lake roads. Cabins were shut, boarded up for winter; ditches and roadsides lay burnt gray-brown from frost and snow, but spring flowers burst through this dreary mantle and punctuated the landscape with color. In the yards and back fields of this tiny encampment, I cut every wild iris I could find, loading arms with my booty—a flower thief. Giddy, I returned to the Big Six and adorned every shelf and counter, my desk, and my bedside table with blooms that were fragile yet alive.

I remember feeling at once home and lost in those first few days, as if my ship had entered harbor for a much-needed respite, but when I disembarked, I did not know what to do with myself on land. Instead, I felt adrift from my life of journeying. In those first days I would gladly have set sail again, motored into the swells of the sea. The gray sky and windless days entombed me, and despite the flowers that filled my house, I believed no life invigorated this landscape. I was unable to sense the power just below the surface of earth. The land was alive with potential, and I touched only an edge of that massive force as it inched into my life.

Two or three days into my visit, I prepared for my first evening walk to the dam, a familiar jaunt at Lake Ericson. The dam sits at the end of the lake road and serves as a destination for people hungry for constitutionals, for lovers wandering the peach-colored sunset, for children captive to the out-of-doors, as I had been. When I set out on this inaugural walk, it was a way of saying, *Yes, I am here; I remember the old patterns; I will now embrace what I remember.*

The light that night was thin and pink in the west and buzzing with insects—not the deep bullfrog summer sound of July, rich with the sweet root smell of cedar soaked with water, but the brisk June night, pristine and haunted by flitting bugs and nighthawks. My memory tells me the hazy cloud that had enveloped the lake until that day had risen, and perhaps the lifting of that veil launched me out into the world.

Near the dam I ran into Derald Watson, my old friend from twenty years before. Hand in hand he walked with a woman he introduced as Jewel. We shared our stories, swatting and flipping hands at mosquitoes, until a gold Chevy Malibu chugged by in low gear and distracted us. Derald and Jewel whispered that the young man hanging from the window, waving and grinning, was Teddi and Bob Spilinek's son. It had been years since I had seen Craig Spilinek, and I did not recognize him in the half light of June 1984.

We stood for long minutes near the falling water of the dam at the south end of Lake Ericson, until pink light of sunset turned into thick gray of dusk. Jewel and Derald told me the news of the town: tales of the Hungry Horse, changes at the Salebarn, the fortunes and misfortunes of various ranchers, business failings, deaths, divorces, marriages, births. I felt I had been gone only a few weeks, not years.

The next day Craig Spilinek showed up at the Big Six. I was outdoors cutting the grass, which had grown tall with the abundant spring rains. Finally it had seemed dry enough to take on, and I inched the mower through the jungle, gnawing off swaths of knee-high grass that then had to be raked into stacks. Craig maneuvered his truck into the yard and backed up to one of the stacks. Springing from the cab, he greeted me as if no time had passed. Damn, he was glad to see me, he said. His eyes showed a kind of appreciation that frightened me. This was the first of many encounters with men in the hills that would confuse me and bring on waves of guilt.

"Let me haul these stacks away for you," he said. How could I refuse? I had no truck or other vehicle that would allow me to take away the towering piles cropping up across the yard. We worked together for the rest of the afternoon, raking, stacking, and heaving. Finally Craig revved the engine of his truck, waved an expansive hand out the window, brown eyes smiling with mischievous pleasure, and with the rear end of his pickup riding the ground, he drove out the gate and around the line of cedars in the west.

Shortly after Craig's visit, my father drove up to the Big Six to see that I had managed all the tasks of opening the cabin, and while I do not recall the intricacies of his visit, I remember in Technicolor one incident: our dinner at the Hungry Horse Saloon.

Famous for its sirloins that lap the edges of plates, for its rowdy dances and good-natured joking, and for its round-buying atmosphere and friendly patrons, the Hungry Horse pulsated in my consciousness like a circus calliope. It was a focal point, a gathering spot, a watering hole, a measure of the tenor of the hills. I had set out to get its story when I left Iowa and graduate school, yet when we walked in the door, I was overwhelmed by its dynamics.

My father stepped to the bar to order a drink, and men from three directions fell our way. Like pins in a bowling alley they tumbled over chairs and companions, all offering to buy me a drink. I remember being appalled. In my mind, I see my father chuckling as if he knows the punch line to some joke. I see a beautiful woman sitting next to a handsome cowboy who wears a black Stetson. The woman continues eating, looking up at me tentatively over her salad while her escort almost climbs the table to be the loudest bidder in the drink-buying war. He wins and insists on buying me a Kahlúa-and-cream. It is good, and he is pleased, smiling at me with chocolate eyes. I feel myself scurrying along behind my father to our table, like a tiny skiff in the wake of a larger boat.

This, then, was my reintroduction to Ericson and the Hungry Horse, and it set the tone for my summer in the hills. I was skittish and frightened by the attention of the cowboys, confused about goals yet determined to write a story. They, the people of Ericson, were fully in their lives, busy, curious, ornery. They expected I would join in their work and play, that I would become one with them in their love of this land and life. I had only to figure out how.

Any description I can give of Ericson will be shadowed by emotional attachment; the place seems large and golden in my mind because of a childhood spent there, because of memories of Mother, because of family, because of history. Even when I try to be objective, Ericson wins me over. There was something wholly different about that place when I was growing up there as a child, and it was not just summer fun. I had plenty of summer fun in Osceola, spending long hours at the swimming pool and wandering the Ridge with my friends Terri Howe and Ann Cerny.

Late one night, sitting at my desk reading old settlement histories of Ericson and Osceola, I searched for the key to what made those towns grow in such different directions. Both offered similar pioneer stories—1860 Scandinavian immigrants, sod houses, Homestead Act claims, hand plows, faded photos of women with starched dresses and grim faces—but finally it dawned on me, the most obvious of elements: the land. Ericson was founded along the Cedar River. Osceola, the seat of Polk County, was purposefully located central in the county. Davis Creek, which in my memory held water only when it flooded in the spring, ran in a hollow between the bluff where Osceola's business district sat and the Ridge, where we lived. The nearest rivers were the Blue, a stream south of town, and the Platte, which formed the northern border of Polk County. In Osceola, the soil was dark and fertile; the county had grown up around farming.

But Ericson . . . Ericson prospered on the banks of the Cedar River. The surrounding land was sandy prairie, and although early settlers hoped they could turn their homesteaded acres to crops, they learned early that prairie hay and cattle were more appropriate. The culture that developed around Ericson was based on ranching. In Osceola it remained focused on the plow. These two ways of life produce very different people—farmers and ranchers. Fundamental differences, rooted in land use, separate these groups, as any history of settlement in the American West will tell. In Nebraska we identify members of each clan by their different hats: Ranchers wear Stetsons; farmers wear seed-corn caps. Add to that basic difference the numbing distances between towns in the hills, the oceanlike atmosphere of living in the dunes, adrift, alone for months on end, waves of grass as one's sole company. No, Ericson and Wheeler County required of their inhabitants a different kind of constitution than fertile, flat Polk County in south-central Nebraska, where settlements were more frequent and the land yielded to man's hand. This was farmland—supple, predictable, pliant. The hills, they had a mind of their own.

But more. Ericson was a destination resort. From the time the first dam was built on the Cedar River south and east of Ericson, the reservoir, or Lake Ericson as it became known, attracted people from around Nebraska, and as its reputation as a bass fishing lake grew, it drew anglers from surrounding states. Duck hunting was popular, too.

Nothing in Osceola made it a destination in the way the lake drew people to Ericson. Certainly, Osceola was the county seat, and that attracted settlers and business to the town. A school was built; farm implement and lumber stores opened, and shops served the burgeoning community. After World War II, GIs flooded back into Osceola with new wives, and the population grew. In the 1950s, the county hospital was located in Osceola and that continued to keep the town alive, but Ericson lived and died as a frontier town. Population peaked in the 1920s, at around three hundred. When the Burlington Northern Railroad pulled out its line in the early 1940s, Ericson was already a fading Sandhills town. That act and the relocation of the highway—a federal effort in the 1960s to streamline traffic across America—from main street Ericson to a new, wider asphalt road north of the hamlet, set the course for a town whose most vibrant history lay in pioneer days, before telephones, before the motorcar became common, before roads were paved in the state. Even before Nebraska celebrated its sixtieth year of statehood, Ericson had met its golden moment and that moment had passed, leaving behind a burnished memory of good times, tough times, times of overcoming the odds—all in the past.

When we began traveling to Ericson in the 1950s and 1960s, I was a child and this was a frontier town. Its spirit was frontier; its identity still lingered in the shadows of history. Old-timers in town told stories of mail delivery by team and buggy from Spalding, twenty-five miles south; of dressed prairie chickens shipped out on the train bound for restaurants in Chicago; and of the Ericson Literary Society, which had met in the Modern Woodmen of America hall, the same building that became the Ericson Bar and Grill and then the Hungry Horse. Instinctively, I had identified something raw about Ericson that did not vitalize Osceola, a town of Swedish origins working hard to meet the twentieth century. No, Ericson was still living in the nineteenth century, and its people were happy for it.

Even in its layout, Ericson resembled an Old West town. While Osceola was built around a courthouse square with a marble edifice filling the city center, Ericson was erected along one street, which entered in the east and shot out the west end. The business area of downtown Ericson was two blocks long, with storefronts facing a street wide enough for angle parking on each side and a row of wagons, or, later, cars and pickups, down the center—a tradition that remains today. Stores were simple frame structures with a single central door opening onto a traditional boardwalk. Benches lined the fronts of shops, and on egg-and-daughter nights—evenings when locals brought eggs, cream, and daughters to town, the eggs and cream for shipment out on the Burlington Northern, the daughters for show—men lined the street smoking pipes and talking politics, and women crowded the shops.

These frontier patterns were common to towns all over Nebraska in the late 1800s and early 1900s, but in Ericson, these days were the town's most vital time. They shadow all other events in Ericson—the heady days of settlement, of possibility, before the land asserted itself and made it clear to the dogmatic Swedes and hardworking Norwegians that this land would not yield to row crop agriculture, a realization that drove many of the original settlers and their children from the area.

The same is true for Osceola, of course, another Nebraska rural town in decline, but Osceola's demise began to show itself later, after my own exodus. My high school class was the largest ever to graduate from Osceola High School. From the 1970s forward, Osceola has seen swift population reductions; businesses have closed, and children have not stayed or returned to raise families, as their parents did after World War II.

In Ericson, though, the peaking and exodus and decline happened much earlier. By the time I arrived on the scene as a child, Ericson was nearly a ghost town, and the ghosts were seductive, whispering the old dreams through the cottonwoods, stories on the wind, in the prairie. This was still, in many ways, old Nebraska.

* * *

It didn't take long for word to get around town that Bill Norton's daughter was living down at the lake, and people began seeking me out, men and women alike. I was the new girl in town, and these Sandhills folk were hungry for something new. Jewel, Derald's companion, whom I had met on my first walk to the dam, began making frequent forays around the sandy bend in the road from her sun-baked trailer to the Big Six. She came with offerings of jelly canned in baby food jars, marching right across the yard and up to the screen door of the back porch. I welcomed her at first, but when her visits became too frequent, I considered nailing to my door the kind of announcement Pasternak once did: "Go Away, I'm Working."

Others came, too. One woman whom I enjoyed immensely, Laura Gordon, made visits throughout my summer in the hills. She was a self-taught woman who had overcome great odds to keep herself alive intellectually, a woman who had lost one daughter to an icy, blind, early-morning car accident, a woman who nurtured her three other daughters to grow beyond the confines of Wheeler County—a place she admitted she loved for the land but that also carried certain pressures: vast distances, few companions, isolation, the seductively soothing effects of alcohol on a family, and the pressure to conform to the mold of conservative rural America.

Our conversations were far-ranging, often theoretical as we danced around the specifics of our own lives, each knowing the implications of her comments, but neither pushing for brazen confessions. We nurtured each other over cups of tea, and I was always happy to see her boat of a car sail into my yard.

Teddi Spilinek and her husband, Bob, lived just east of the Big Six in a house originally owned by Teddi's parents, Felix and Pat Geisinger. Teddi had grown up in Nebraska, as had Bob, but when they married, Bob was in the Navy, and they were stationed in San Diego. Later, after Bob retired and Teddi's parents died, leaving behind a house, the family moved back to Nebraska and the hills.

Teddi was tolerant; I never felt she judged me for my differences. In fact, she may have liked me more for them. While many of

Ericson's characters seemed interested in me, I sensed that to most, I was little more than passing fascination, a shiny trinket. Not so with the Spilineks. I always sensed their reliability; it was like a pact, a bond, never spoken, simply known. To me, Teddi was family.

When I set out to tell this story of the summer of 1984, I laid out several eight-inch-by-eleven-inch sheets of paper, end to end, taping them where they joined. Then I drew a long line in pencil that traversed each of the sheets.

"This is my life," I said.

At the left end of the line I made a tick mark and wrote in tiny script "Arrival" and added an approximate date. At the far right end I wrote "Leaving" and another date. What lay in between was a blank. Oh, I could remember highlights, but the images that came were fuzzy around the edges; they seemed to blend into and out of a big gray cloud. Each memory flashed like a bolt of lightning— from where it emanated could not be traced; to what it pointed there was no clue. I laboriously hauled out all my old research notes, copies of letters, and journal entries and began the tedious and somewhat uncomfortable process of putting that summer into a chronology. I tried to coordinate dates from the various sources so that I could get a sense of time's flow. At best, though, the result was like an old crank car, jumping and jolting its way forward. Finally, after some work, I had a series of tick marks along the time line of my life. Those above the line represented efforts to complete my master's project; those below the line represented deviations, or so I thought. In the end, there were a lot more marks below the line. This disturbed me. I lived my life wrong, I thought. I can't tell this story. But of course it is the very story I have to tell—the story of how I stumbled into the future with only a vague blueprint as guide—because it was the unexpected, the unplanned events of this journey that in the end taught me the most.

*   *   *

One of the first marks on the time line was a spring cattle auction at the Salebarn and the party at the Hungry Horse that followed. I remember it because it was my initiation; it was the first time I rode the horse.

Cattle auctions are held at the Ericson Livestock Commission Company, or the Salebarn, as locals know it, throughout the year. Many cattlemen sell portions of their herds after a summer of grazing, because cows are heavier then and will bring more money on the sale block. Ranchers also sell cattle in the fall to avoid feeding them during the winter. In spring, ranchers buy bulls and heifers to fill out herds for summer grazing. Older cows and heifers that don't produce are "going to town," or the slaughterhouse.

Whatever the case was that spring, the sale at the Ericson Salebarn in June 1984 was a big one, with people in town from all over the hills. I took my camera to the Salebarn—it's north of town, along Highway 91/70—and prepared to capture the event on film.

The Salebarn consists of a large metal two-story building that holds the sale arena, business office, and Ranch Café. Behind the complex stretches a web of holding pens, chutes, and alleyways, all constructed from lumber and once painted white. They push up into the prairie dunes that back the barn. No trees shelter this area, and a huge gravel parking lot reaches from the front door to the highway. On sale days, the lot is filled with semitrailers, Ford pickups, Buicks, Chryslers, horse trailers, and Cadillacs from all over the hills.

For days before a Saturday sale, truckers will back their cattle trucks up to the loading docks, and rivers of bawling cattle will tumble down the gangplanks and into a corral. From there they will be divided and herded into a number of the one hundred and fifty holding pens. If the sale is a big one, by Friday night there will be so many cattle in the holding pens that you can hear them bawling into the starlit night, all the way down the River Road at the Big Six.

On this particular day hundreds of Hereford, Black Baldy, Angus, and Charolais cattle were waiting in pens for the sale, which would begin before noon and last until late in the day. With my thirty-five-millimeter camera and several rolls of film, I crawled all over the web of plankways that snake out above the network of pens, shooting images of cows and ranchers, cowboys driving cattle down alleys below me, and horseback riders cracking switches over the heads and on the rumps of reluctant cows.

Inside, men and women in jeans and boots huddled and sprawled in the bleachers surrounding the ring. Cigarette smoke hung in the air. Small aluminum pie plates scattered throughout the bleachers served as ashtrays. A brood of active children climbed over parents and patrons, chasing each other to the top of the bleachers, where they compared their boots. The auctioneer's voice hummed along at a consistent drone, punctuated by: "Come on boys. Now, these are good cows!"

Sandhills ranchers are famous for both reticence and bullish banter, which they fluctuate back and forth between, depending on how well they know you. By the end of the afternoon I was acquainted with a good portion of the men at the sale, although I remember little of our conversations. What I do remember was the heady feeling of being there: the hills rippling off in every direction, a strong southwest wind raking my skin, handsome men, and my camera keeping the distance between us. I felt safe when I carried my camera; it set me apart, legitimized my appearance, and in some unspoken way said: Hands off.

The next image in my mind is the view of the bar through the door of the Hungry Horse. Several years ago the Ericson Bar and Grill was remodeled by a new owner. Out front he constructed a classic boardwalk with an overhanging roof supported by wooden pillars. It is from this boardwalk that I contemplate the interior of the Hungry Horse Saloon.

The sunlight is a warm yellow and the door is propped open onto the boardwalk and street. Inside cowboys in jeans and snap-button shirts with Stetsons and cowboy boots lean against the bar. They fill every seat at the round corner table and perch on stools. Long-neck beer bottles clink; barefoot children wander in and out the door. Women in spaghetti-strap tops and tight jeans gather at another table. I immediately spot the two best-looking boys in the bunch. Later I learn they are the Kaster boys—dangerously hand-some and charming. One is engaged to a slip of a girl, athletic and blond; the other already has a live-in, strikingly beautiful, tall, thin, fine-boned. I soon learn that none of that matters.

I shoot a few images of this view—the cowboys and their long-neck beers, the pool table and the late-afternoon early-summer light, the children, the women with husbands parked at tables in corners of the room, a roomful of faces I do not know. Years later these images will serve as a touchstone to take me back to the stories of that summer; each face will evoke a series of interactions, conversations, moments that together constitute my knowledge of a place called the Hungry Horse Saloon.

I can't remember if I tumbled of my own free will through the door frame and into the rising party or if some good-natured thirsty soul gave me a shove, but once I was through the door, the ride picked up speed. I found a stool at the bar and ordered a beer. The bartender—one of those Kaster boys and the same cowboy who bought my first drink at the Hungry Horse—wouldn't take my money. Someone else had bought my Bud, he said. Parched from the hot afternoon, I gulped the first few swallows. Before I could even finish the bottle, another appeared in its place, then another and another. I never bought one beer that afternoon or evening.

The cowboys were greasing their creaking social skills; anxious to talk to me, they crowded round. Cowhands and order buyers from the Salebarn trailed in after work, and the place was filling up—two hundred people, maybe more, standing, sitting, flowing in and out the door into the cooling air of a June night. Some moved to restaurant tables through the swinging doors and ordered sirloins or T-bone steaks, hash browns, and tossed salad. I never left the saloon. I should have eaten, but the liquor seemed to fill the hungry place inside me, that and the crazy flow of friendliness that engulfed me.

I struck up an in-depth conversation with an order buyer, a man who bought cattle for the packing house, a man old enough to be my father, a man I now realize was also hitting on me as I listened and analyzed his life, but I didn't think of that, sitting there in the rowdy Hungry Horse, George Jones blaring from the jukebox, the smell of beefsteak hanging in the air. No, I thought of little but the man's story and the quenching flow of beer, in a place that felt like home and yet felt foreign and evocative in ways I could not identify.

My next memory is of me sitting on the bar. It is dark outside and there is talk of a party at the Blue Rocks—a typical jaunt from the Hungry Horse to a skeet-shooting range at the lake after the bar closes down, rather like the high school parties I remember from growing up in Nebraska, circling the cars in some anonymous field, like wagons on the trail. Someone cranks up the stereo and the keg is tapped. The Blue Rocks was no different. The crowd was just older.

Next, I see myself in the arms of some tall cowboy. I remember being chilled. I must have worn only a light shirt. He is gentle and warms me. I am very drunk. Later, I will not even remember his face and always wonder which out of the crowd of poker-faced cowhands was the big, careful man.

I wake up in my bunk in the Big Six the next morning with my head pounding and spinning. I haul a lounger out into the yard and flop onto it, letting the sun bake me awake. I still wear my nightgown.

A car rumbles up outside the picket fence; a voice calls out: "How 'bout heading into the Horse. Little of what got you will do you good."

I prop myself on an elbow. It's that handsome cowboy, one of the Kasters—the one with a woman already in his house. He's leaning on the fence, looking down at me appreciatively, lean hips, brown eyes, black hat.

I decline.

He wants to banter, and so we do, me in my nightgown stretched on a chaise lounge in the middle of a prairie-grass-tufted yard, primly surrounded by a white picket fence, in the midst of twenty thousand square miles of sandy hills, on the edge of a life I cannot predict, with a smooth-talking cowboy the dimensions of whose charm I cannot even fathom.

In time he drives on, gunning his engine a little as he moves slowly away from the fence. I feel safe and sick and overwhelmed by the events of the day before, most of which I cannot remember. I vow to clean up my act, and wander back into the Big Six to scramble three eggs and fry four slices of bacon. I eat everything, including two pieces of toast. I shower. My head throbs. It takes an entire day to recover. I steer clear of the Hungry Horse for days, having learned my lesson. One ride on that bucking horse was enough.

I drive to Ord in Valley County and visit the library, where I check out several books on local history. The Nebraska library system has a liberal interlibrary loan policy, and the librarian is happy to help me conduct research. In time, I request books and journal articles from all over the state, many coming from the University of Nebraska Libraries in Lincoln.

I spend the next few days atoning for my sins. I work in the office I have created in the east bedroom of the Big Six, a section of porch my father walled off to make a bedroom for my brother when we grew too old to share a room. It is a narrow room, perhaps six feet wide and twelve feet long. The east and south walls are lined with screened windows that run directly above my desk. I read articles and make notes in my journal with no sense of where I am headed with this project.

I also set about the business of reacquainting myself with the lake. I walk to the Point, where Billy and I once held our late-night jumping competitions. No open sand remains; it is overgrown by willow bushes. The beach, too, has been transformed. Two years before, a wall of water surged down the river, pushed across the lake in one great sweep, and smashed into the half-moon beach. It completely demolished the sandy bank where I played with childhood friends, and the force of water reshaped the gently sloping bed of the lake. No longer is it a safe place to play, and someone has strung a fence blocking entry to the path that leads to the beach.

I wander the north end of the lake, where the shimmering white sand island once sprouted from the waters of the Cedar. It has become a thriving marsh, overgrown with cattails and reed canary grass. When the dew still grips the bunchgrass, I move through first light, camera in hand, snapping images of boats on sawhorses, of sections of docks stacked along the banks of the lake, of lean-to sheds with elm sticks shoved through latches to act as locks, of abandoned cabins and trailers hemmed by cottonwoods, with golden hills stretching forever behind them into the clear blue light of morning.

These were the details that girded the lake of my youth, and unconsciously I was compiling a visual record of these images to augment my memory pictures of a place to which I would return again and again in my life, looking for something missing, looking for the essence of a place, some volatile I could bottle, carry with me into the unknown future, some magical potion that would buoy me back to the safety of childhood and would, like a heady whiff of camphor, infuse me with the balm of a healing remedy.

I steer a wide path around the Hungry Horse for weeks. If I go there at all I go only during the day, to visit with Clarence or his son, Stan, who operate the place. Both are tall, narrow, elastic-faced fellows with ready grins, and I develop a pattern of stopping in during early afternoon, after the lunch crowd but before the local boys get off work and come by for a beer. I hang on the corner stool near the stack of Omaha *World Herald* newspapers and act as if I am reading. Every once in a while I ask a question, or Clarence will offer a tidbit. He says his family ran another place in Litchfield, south and west of Ericson, for a number of years. Stan says he and his wife live in a place halfway between Ericson and Ord. Wilma, Clarence's wife, runs the kitchen. By stopping at the Hungry Horse and visiting, I come to believe that I am indeed working on my project, even though I have no idea what information I am seeking.

Sometime in June my father calls and suggests I invite my mother to the lake to spend some time at the Big Six. It is a shocking, generous, and curious idea. My mother has not been in the cabin since the early 1970s. I have not been with her in that space in almost fifteen years. I cannot comprehend my father's thinking. I call her, though, and lay out the invitation.

Why yes, she likes that idea. She thinks she will come. I am in a dither: How will I ever wipe away the years of dirt and clutter? How will I ever present to her the place she worked so hard to create? Years of neglect and my father's dictum of "Throw nothing away" have transformed our beloved Big Six into a dusty flea market, nothing like the ship my mother used to run. Certainly I have cleaned. I had opened the cabin in the traditional way, removing everything from the cupboards, scrubbing and polishing, and yet in the end it still looks worn; the mishmash of furnishings don't create a whole, a place that gels in my mind as a tidy, tasteful space.

I call my mother and lay out the truth. She agrees to simply not look. I await her arrival with excitement and fear. My mother in the Big Six! What I have desired for so long is about to transpire.

The next image is of my mother draped over the couch that takes up the reading corner of the front porch, a place two stately wooden rockers used to occupy. The very fact that my mother is in the reclining position is novel. She is a woman who rarely rests, from the time she rises in the morning until the time she tumbles into bed at night. "Activity." "Lists." "Organization." These are words that define my mother, but here, for this brief moment, she has decided to drape herself over the tiny couch, propped up by pillows, listening to wren song, watching the long yellow rays of afternoon sun stretch out from the western horizon, blast through the cottonwoods, and bake the grass in the yard. It is no longer her home. All the fussing, tidying, and cleaning she once would have done are inappropriate now. Instead, perhaps for the first time, she simply lets herself *be* in this place. It is a mystifying time for me. I don't know how to act. I have become the woman of the house. Who is this woman with me?

I have packed in a stack of *New Yorker* magazines, and we hole up on the front porch, reading articles and talking. Cowboys drive by and gun their engines. My mother is amused. I am embarrassed. I am trying to be a good girl, yet still the cowboys come. Craig Spilinek drives in with a bowl of strawberries. Another cowboy wants me to drink beer with him at the Hungry Horse. He is polite to my mother and she is charmed. She does not understand the confusion that tumbles inside me. Even though she was the first person I called that night four years ago when I was raped, it is clear she does not comprehend the contradictions that now plague my soul, and I am unable to talk about them.

Our culture lays the blame for the crime of rape at the woman's feet. The first question always asked is "What were you doing there?" or "What were you wearing?"—as if a woman does not have the right to move on this planet, as if a woman does not have the right to choose the clothes she will wear, as if a man is not responsible for his own actions. It took me over a decade to separate out that part of the incident which was my responsibility, to recognize that I was not guilty in the ways society would have me believe. During the summer of 1984, four short years after I was attacked, I was still far from understanding that I did not provoke that man's behavior. Instead, I felt guilty if any man showed interest in me. It was a simple equation: If a man showed interest, I must have done something to bring it on, and that was bad, because if you attracted a man's interest, he would hurt you, and it would be your own fault.

My attacker's responsibility didn't even enter the equation for me back then, and he was never caught, so whatever questions I might have addressed by facing him in a courtroom were never raised. Instead, I limped forward, unsure of why my life had unfolded the way it had, and doubtful I could repair the gaping wounds I struggled to conceal.

All that confusion was combined with questions from my past still unresolved: my parents' divorce and my mother's exit from my life. Returning to Ericson brought all this back, like a movie playing continuously on the inside of my forehead—images, words, scenes all swirling around, and me in the midst of it trying to entertain my mother in the house that had once been a sacred space for our family, where once I had been the girl draped across the couch.

A series of color snapshots I saved tell me we drove down the River Road together. In the images, my mother wears cutoffs, a long-sleeved T-shirt, dark glasses, and tennis shoes. She holds a bunch of dried grasses snipped from a ditch, and a pair of scissors. I recall we hauled our collection back to the Big Six and made several arrangements that we tucked into jars and planted on tables.

We visited Bob Spilinek's hardware store in Ericson. He kept behind the counter a shoe box full of less-than-tasteful birthday cards, and my mother, who with a small group of women friends shared a tradition of sending such cards on birthdays, was seeking something different. I recall little of what was said that day, but I remember well my mother bantering with Bob. I see her head tossing back, her mouth opening, and that big, round laugh popping out into the room—her trademark behavior. Right after that laugh, the chin comes down, the fingers lift the cigarette, and she takes a long drag, blowing smoke up and to the left with the follow-up chortle.

In this series of movements a mélange of years and parties tumbles by me, and always my mother laughs and smiles; people draw near her laugh. She is a woman who will remain attractive every day of her life, because she has the rare capacity to enliven a place. Quick with words and jokes, she molds around her a world of gaiety and beauty, laughter and ideas. Standing in Bob's shop, I see the old pattern playing out. She smiles right at him, listens, follows up his jokes with her own, and charms him in a way most women could not imagine. I am in awe of her ease in social situations and find myself wanting to hook my mittens to her jacket and wander along behind quietly, listening.

Next door, Ellie in Pat's Market is delighted to see my mom. They talk as if fifteen years have not intervened. My mother buys cigarettes and we hit upon the idea of taking back to the Big Six a pack of windmill cookies—the kind my mother bought in summer when the cookie jar ran low. Nowhere else have I ever had these cookies; they are an artifact of my past, of the lake and the Big Six Country Club. We pace the dark aisles of the tiny store, searching. At the same instant we spot the package, and as our hands shoot out in unison, reaching for the familiar, flat, cellophane-covered pack, both of our heads flash back, spontaneously, red hair shaking over our shoulders, and a common laugh erupts. It is an instant of quiet knowledge that passes quickly but that I savor for years.

We stop at the Hungry Horse for a beer. Dave Howard, one of the Hungry Horse regulars, is there, and he and my mother talk as if they had just seen each other last summer. I keep waiting for the words I hear in my head: "My God, Nancy, there you are. Why, we've missed you!" But no one says this, and I am disappointed they do not seem to realize the weightiness of this moment.

Back at the cabin, a couple of final moments spin out to complete my mother's visit. I have no recollection, though, of the matter that hangs them together. Instead, I see only two bright images, hanging in space.

My father has been working as a judge during these years. Four or five years after my mother left, he was appointed to the bench. He is a district judge and conducts business in Polk, Butler, and Sanders counties. Sometimes, though, he travels to other parts of the state to hear cases. It is on one of these journeys that he turns up at the cabin. I suppose we know he is coming. I suppose we are ready when his red Cougar turns the corner beyond the cedars and eases into the yard. Perhaps there has been some prior planning of what we will do when my father arrives at the Big Six, when my mother is there, when I am there, the daughter of these two people who together saw a vision of what this ramshackle hull of a home could be. I suppose all this because I cannot remember. Instead, I see my father step through the back screen door. My mother and I stand between the kitchen and the back porch. I am aware of the cottonwood fuzz on the screens, of the color of light and the sweet cedar smell in the air. He is carrying something; it is a kitten. My mother simply observes, one arm wrapped around her waist. The other holds a cigarette.

I watch the look on my father's face as he enters this tiny room, his past wife standing there with the daughter of that union, and he reminds me of a little boy bringing home for the first time some found object, some treasure for a loved one. There are tears in the edges of his eyes—he is a sentimental man beneath his gruff exterior. He is reaching out his arm with this little tuft of fur in it, handing it to me.

"Here," he says. "I thought you needed a cat." I can feel my mother summing up my father's actions as ill-planned, but he is so genuine. I hurt to see the contrast of their approaches to living exposed in the same room.

"Well, Nancy," he says, turning toward her. "It's nice to see you here." The look in his dewy eyes is of love. My mother's left arm draws more tightly around her waist. She drags on her cigarette.

"Good grief, Bill," she says. "A kitten."

"She followed me back to my motel room," he offers guiltily, like a kid caught in the act of something forbidden.

In my mind I see him turning to this little animal and calling, "Here kitty, here kitty," as it stands on the curb of some dusty Sandhills town, mewing and pleading for attention. Of course it follows him back to his motel. He begs it to follow. He goes immediately to the grocery and buys cat food and litter. An old softie with too many strays already populating his life, he plans to make a family for me.

My mother is not amused, and I recognize a familiar tenor in her attitude toward my father. Had I known this dynamic as a child?

They move swiftly to the great room of the cabin, my father setting down his briefcase. My mother slides open the cupboard to reach for the bottle of scotch that has for all time resided on the bottom shelf under the counter.

I'm not sure how long my father stays. I'm not sure what I do with the rest of my time while he is there. I'm not sure if I have a drink, too. The only thing I remember about my mother's visit after that encounter is a single moment.

I am standing by the sink in the kitchen, a spot from which I can see into the bedroom that was once my parents'. At the end of my view stand my mother and father. My mother is cupping something in her hands. I do not know what. She is facing me but does not see me. Instead, with chin dipped, she is looking from the object in her hands to my father. He stands with his back toward me, yet I see the outline of his face. He is looking down at my mother.

In an instant, a flash of memory, I see a group of images in a photo album. They are of my mother and father, who have just married, or perhaps they are engaged, or are still college students, standing in the yard of my mother's parents' home in Lincoln, Nebraska. In the series of photos, my mother wears a calf-length skirt and plaid Pendleton jacket; my father wears a long-sleeved dress shirt and baggy pants. It is fall in the late 1940s.

In one image my grandpa Dale rakes leaves in a border along the house; in another my mother poses with her mother, Lucille. In the final image—the one that has emblazoned itself on my memory and rises here today in this cabin in these wandering hills, hundreds of miles and thirty-five years away from that moment, a moment before I was even born—my mother leans against a tree, one leg bent at the knee, the sole of her foot flat against the trunk. My father stands beside her, much as they stand today in this bedroom. He looks down at her, she up at him, and the look across time is identical: flirtatious.

I am dumbfounded and a wave of emotion hits me like a breaker rolling in off a winter sea. I have to reach for the counter to steady myself. She looks up at him coyly; he smiles with desire. I have to walk away. I never tell anyone what has happened.

Days later my mother is gone. My father has returned to his work in Wahoo, where he dispenses justice for the Fifth Judicial District of Nebraska. I call the county extension agent in Burwell to talk about Sandhills prairie. A woman answers the phone. She offers to take me out into the land the following week, to talk about grasses and range management. I put my mother's and father's coinciding visit behind me, filing it with other unmanageable moments on some shelf of my memory, in a box labeled "My Life," a box growing full, a box which I am not yet ready to open.

I meet the county extension agent at her office in Burwell. She is about my age, recently graduated from agricultural school at the University of Nebraska, about five and a half feet tall, with black hair clipped short; she's wearing jeans and boots. She slips on a light jacket and suggests we take her truck. The seat is dusty and covered with papers, which she pushes into a pile, then steers the truck east and into the hills north of Burwell, turning off Highway 11 onto a back road.

I tell her I am finishing a graduate degree at the University of Iowa, writing a story about Ericson, the Sandhills, and the Hungry Horse Saloon. "I need to know more about ranching," I say, a vague request, which only increases the awkwardness I feel in her presence. She is directed, stable, and I sense about her something I do not have: a clear sense of her place in the world.

I ask questions about plants we pass and she explains the differences between grasses cattle like and those they avoid. She talks about winter pasture, summer pasture, and overgrazing.

I am not a rancher's daughter and a lot of the talk goes above my head. I have never thought of cattle as a commodity, as a product you grow, weighing the expense of feed against weight gain, against market price per pound, against the unknown winter weather, against the quality of a given area of rangeland to sustain a herd. Terms like "heifer," "feeder cattle," and "steer" are mysterious. I wish I had the key to enter this private world of prairie and a life on the land, but I am an outsider. That I cannot change. Still, I pump her for facts, which I record diligently in a reporter's notebook, a notebook I will lose later during a time when I let winds blow me in a different direction, guided by some greater force toward understanding.

Sometime during that first month I make another trip into backcountry, with Dick Foster, the father of my childhood Ericson friend Dixie Foster. Dixie was short and solid, wore sensible glasses and a pixie haircut. She was a star student, played the piano, knew how to sew, and rode a horse the way I always dreamed: as part of the hide of the horse, close to bone and mane and tail. She leaned over the neck of her pony, Traveler, became an integral part of prairie, moved through landscape, pounding dirt.

Sometimes Dixie and I dressed in swimming suits and tennis shoes and walked the quarter mile from the Foster ranch down the gravel road to the wooden bridge that crossed the Cedar River. We made up imaginary lives there, casting ourselves as improbable characters, then acting out the roles. Dixie was a city woman, powerful and alluring, a femme fatale. I was a Hollywood star, sleek, sophisticated, with a purring voice. We strutted back and forth across the worn planks, frogs echoing our lines, and did our best on those summer afternoons to dream ourselves right out of Wheeler County. Then we pushed a path through willows down to the shallow, sandy river and hooted at families of swallows nesting under the bridge, waving our arms and watching with open mouths and tilted heads the great waves of wings that arched out, banked, and fluttered back. Their flight was our dream, to propel ourselves away from the languid, horsefly-filled Sandhills afternoons and into some bigger, more important world, full of action and fancy talk. I could not have known that my flight would mirror so closely the arching journey of those swallows—out and up, curving gracefully; the momentary sense of hovering indecision; then the quick descent home.

While Dixie now worked in banking in the northeast corner of the state, I was back in Ericson, tramping the old trails, driving my car into this familiar lane on an early summer morning, watching the man I knew only as Dixie's father walk from the house, a man who spoke little during my visits but who had been gregarious and funny on the occasional times my parents invited him, his wife, Bonnadel, and Dixie to the Big Six for a dinner of steak and salad. I can still see Dick Foster, a hardy, lean man planted in the middle of the couch at the Big Six, cowboy hat by his side, sandy hair parted and slicked back, a glass of whiskey resting on his knee. His neck and face above the collar of his freshly pressed shirt are wind- and sun-burned, and he is on a roll, telling the stories that wait inside him, that wait to be heard. He looks as if he will erupt with laughter, the skin pulling taut over his lean face as he reels out the story, but instead he is perfectly controlled, the pacing of the story pristine, the pauses placed to win effect. It is my father, instead, who erupts with laughter. He and my mother chortle and rock in their chairs.

Later my father will tell me Dick was with the forces that took Utah Beach in the invasion of Normandy during World War II. I do not understand the depth of what that means until many years later, and certainly long after this moody June morning when Dick strides out the door of the Foster ranch, a feather jutting from the crown of his hat. He carries a beer in one hand. His legs are slightly bowed.

Dick Foster grew up in Ericson, one of ten children of a Burlington Northern section boss. He has lived his entire life in the hills around Ericson, except for his years of military service. He motions to the cab of his truck. As long as I can remember, Dick Foster has driven white pickups with red letters riding the tailgate: F O R D. We slide in on opposite sides of the cab. Dick cranks the engine and we bump out the drive and across the rickety plank bridge spanning the Cedar on the dump road. The morning is heavy with spring fog. The hills, though, are as green as shamrocks. The clouds hug the voluptuous toss of earth and everything seems close, the air tight. We push south through a morning when the rest of the world seems asleep. A trail of gravel dust rises behind the truck.

Dick swerves into a ranch house lane. He tells me it is the old home place, the frame house his father built to replace the soddie Dick was born in.

"I grew up here," he says.

He is a man of few words, yet he answers directly each question I pose, and I have lots of them. Each time he refers to some aspect of ranching I do not understand—about irrigation, or windmills, or salt licks, or pasture, or market price—I ask another question, and he answers forthrightly. With this man, I do not feel embarrassed by my ignorance.

The home place is still in good condition. His brother, Dee, lived there until just recently, he tells me. Then he had to move to town—just too old. "Couldn't manage by himself so far out," Dick says.

Access to the cottonwood-shaded house and outbuildings is cut off now by a fence across the drive. It looks like a place of generations of stories that will soon be lost. I wonder who planted the trees. Dick's parents were some of the first to settle in this area south of Ericson, but back then there were no trees; the land was a sea of grass. In whose imagination did these arching trunks first sprout?

Dick knows where a soddie still stands, and he knows, perhaps better than I, that this is the kind of thing I need to see. It is small, cottagelike, with two rooms—a bedroom and a main room containing the kitchen. Cupboards droop toward the floor, and varieties of wallpaper peel from the walls, layer upon layer of flowers and understated designs signaling the years and generations of hope that once inhabited these rooms. Cattle have been allowed to wander in and out the door and the room is soiled with manure. Only a few windows break the monotony of the walls and they are small. The floor is dirt.

Not far in the future, soddies will be entirely the province of memory and museum reconstruction. These were among the first houses of the people who settled my home state. Soddies followed the dugout—a home like a rat hole, dug into the side of a hill, windowless, with dirt floors and ceilings that shed dust daily. Soddies were a step up; they were the solution for a landscape where no trees grew. The earth itself was cut into blocks and stacked like bricks to build a home. Later inhabitants applied wallpaper and paint to brighten the interior. Soddies were simple, humble homes, rough places tended by women who had once lived in proper frame houses in settled areas like Illinois and Ohio, women who moved west, leaving behind pianos and churches and quilting circles.

Dick keeps to the back roads, paths and trails of sand I did not even know existed. He parks at the top of a hill and we walk down to a graveyard nestled between dunes. A fence surrounds the headstones, but no road approaches. We climb through the wire and read the names: Brown, O'Connor, Gion. Dick moves his arm in the direction of a huddle of trees in the distance. That's the site of the Brown place, he thinks. Nothing now but trees. A light breeze moves the grass. There is little to say. These were Nebraska's pioneers, Sandhills hopefuls, people who came to this prairie from Norway and Sweden, from Holland and Germany, from Iowa and Illinois, people who built soddies and dug wells before Wheeler County was even registered on the books. What remains now of their bold forays into untried land are abandoned homesites, perhaps a few descendants, and trees, blessed cottonwoods.

We drive across prairie for the rest of our journey, avoiding real roads. Dick pushes though bluestem and grama right up to a barbed-wire fence, shifts into park and climbs out with a couple of tools. He pulls out the staples that hold the wire to the fencepost, lays the wire on the ground, steps back into the cab of the Ford, drives over the fencing, then parks again and climbs out to reposition the wires. We move freely across the land this way for hours, and for the first time in my life I have the sense of open prairie before the time of fences, before settlers moved into the Sandhills and the range wars began.

We swing by a herd of Foster cattle to check a salt lick. Dick rumbles a new one out of the truck bed, dropping it on the ground near a windmill and horse tank full of water. He turns. There is the slightest smile pulling at his lips. "Want to see my ponies?"

"You bet."

He crests a dune, drives at an angle down its face through a gully and up the face of another rise. You have to be in these hills to realize how much they undulate. From the road you can see the roll of the land, but to know the chaotic jumble of knots, dips, knolls, and yucca bunches that is these hills, you have to be in the middle of them. I've read that some of the hills rise to five hundred feet, but that doesn't mean much to me until Dick crests a dune and the ground drops away. What lies below is obscured by grass. To ride in a pickup over this crest, to feel your body pitching forward the way it does on a gravity-defying carnival ride, to brace your legs against the floor of the cab, your arms against the armrest, to jostle from left to right, to bounce toward the ceiling and windshield all in one careening twirl, is to know the lay of this land, to touch the edge of mystery these hills presented to pioneers who pushed westward, to know the terror that overcame settlers left alone around the soddie for days or weeks or months on end with nothing but wind and dunes as companion.

We push up the next rise almost in a straight line; no switchback climbing this time. My spine presses against the backrest. Dick guns the engine and I am pushed back like a passenger on takeoff. The truck bounces through sandy holes and around tufts of bunchgrass. At the top, Dick pivots the wheel to the left and we ride the spine of this narrow sandhill. Dick rolls to a halt and cuts the engine. Across on the next hill I see a herd of horses.

"We'll walk," he says. A light rain has begun to fall. I open the cab door, slip to the ground. Together we work through grama and bunchgrass up the next hill. The horses are moving away from us. Dick stops. "Pretty, aren't they?"

It's the kind of question that doesn't need a response.

"They're wild. Appaloosas. Truest line of Indian pony left."

I do not have to ask if he plans to break them. The herd grazes lazily, swishing tails, stomping hooves. All the while, each horse keeps a watchful eye on us. We are miles from civilization, miles from even the smallest of shops, and I feel the clean separation from worldly concerns. A profound isolation injects my veins. This is a landscape bigger than anything I imagined from my Iowa City lookout.

I fall into a pattern with the newest member of my family, Brit the kitty. She is tiny and needy and seems to have missed out on a few of the feline skills mother cats are supposed to teach their young. She climbs the narrow trunks of the maples and elms my father has planted in the yard and waits in the branches to be rescued. Each morning she climbs the mammoth Siberian elm that grows near the back stoop of the Big Six, follows the branches that arch over the roof, leaps onto the shingles, then waits above the back door to be lifted down by warm human hands. I have to stand on tippy toes to reach the roof. Daily a neighbor across the road awaits this ritual. I wear a shortie nightgown, and I wonder if he can see my panties, but he is an old man, and I imagine he has not the eyesight to pick up the details. Still, every morning he hovers at the side of his cabin to watch as I reach to the roof to help Brit down.

Mr. Isakson perpetually wears denim overalls; he frets about his yard, mowing, trimming, and fertilizing daily. His ditches are pruned to perfection. His borders are weedless. His sidewalks are edged. Inside, his wife, Myrna, dies of cancer. I hear this news from Teddi Spilinek, and I decide to begin waving to Mr. Isakson. He returns my gesture. Later I wander over to visit with Myrna, who seems calm in her fate. I do not know death of this kind; I am unfamiliar with lingering, haunting death. The only death I have tasted was death at the hands of another, the man who attacked me—how swift I know it to be, how ephemeral the act of breathing, how fleeting this state we call life, and yet here before my eyes wastes Myrna Isakson. I make light conversation; I help her laugh; she helps me with my confusion in her calm, stately march toward the brink. I go home feeling sad, and much later, for months after I leave Ericson, I write to Mr. and Mrs. Isakson, friendly notes about my travels and about how much I miss the lake. Later I hear in a letter from Teddi that Myrna has encouraged her husband to strike up a friendship with an old high school sweetheart who lives in a town nearby. She has been widowed. The next letter carries the news of Myrna's death. The next of Mr. Isakson's marriage to his old sweetheart. I hear later he has sold his cabin on the banks of Lake Ericson and moved to Arizona to be with this new woman in a place she retains from an earlier life. I wonder how he can leave this sandy land of marsh shallows and great blue herons and mead-owlarks, and then I remember Myrna and her patient preparation for death, and I realize it is because of strength like hers that we must go on; we honor her graceful dance toward the end of her life by choosing the best lives we can imagine. Mr. Isakson's best life has taken him south. I never see him again.

That Kaster boy, the one with the live-in girlfriend, drives by my place a lot. If he sees me on the porch or in the yard, or by chance catches me out for a walk, he stops to chat. I know what he wants. I know he could as easily drive the gravel River Road into town, completely avoiding the slower, sandy loop that dips south off the county road and into the north end of Lake Ericson. I know what's on his mind, and while somewhere inside myself I am flattered by his attention, I am angered by the double standard he deals his woman at home. I feel best when he calls to me from beyond the picket fence, such an incongruity in these hills. Never in my travels from the western end of the Sandhills to the eastern ridge, from the Platte River to the South Dakota border, have I seen another white picket fence. It is my father's way of setting himself apart.

I didn't like the look at first. The old Big Six was bordered by a sagging wire fence I adored. It was unpretentious, ancient, soft but sure in its delineation. It was the fence of my childhood, the fence that greeted me when I ran home from adventures with cousin Miles or brother Billy. It was the fence I associated with home and family. Later my father fell in love with the idea of the high-maintenance picket fence. Every other year it had to be scraped and painted. I thought this was a poor decision, but this summer something about that picket fence comforts me. Its preposterous marching across the landscape says "Keep Out" in a proper New England kind of way, and I appreciate the fact that the architecture can say what I cannot find the words to express.

At night, after the bar closes, a pattern develops, which plays out through the summer. The sound of a truck wakes me as it rumbles by the Big Six, its engine jamming into the quiet of night. It slows right outside the cabin, revs, rumbles on. Some nights it comes by a second time. I begin feeling frightened, alone in the dark, feeling that in the black of night a picket fence is hardly protection against a desirous and drunken cowboy. I lock the screen doors, knowing full well they are little protection against a man who wants in. I lie still in the bunk, nestled in the oldest of cotton sheets, cool air wafting in the windows, watching stars and waiting for the awful sounds of a powerful engine stilling near the Big Six, of hard-soled boots on the walk out front, of someone working the locks, but they never come. Still, when I drift off, chaotic images race through first sleep, of pursuit and strange places and omnipresent threat, and I wake in a panic, breathless, running, a hand close behind, reaching, stretching for my shoulder, whirling me around, catapulting me through space, flying, spinning, out of control. . . .

My journalistic training has taught me that when studying a community, looking for a story, one ought to explore the role of religion. It's rather like conducting an anthropological study of some unknown tribe; one must determine the place of spirit in the lives of the people.

When we were kids we went regularly to Sunday school, which I liked for the stories, and then reluctantly to worship services at the Methodist Church in Osceola with my mother, who steered us to the balcony, handed us a fistful of crayons, paper for doodling, and hymnals as tiny desks. We kept up this pretense until one morning when my parents turned to Billy and me and asked if we wanted to go to church. "No," we chorused. "Fine," they said, and we never went again. Later, in college, I stayed as far away from organized religion as I could get, branding it the antithesis of the logical, rational form of study I pursued.

Yet despite this lack of personal connection with prayer and fellowship, I feel compelled to visit an Ericson church while the locals are at worship. I fear my study will be incomplete if I skirt this aspect of Ericson life, and so I pin down the time of Sunday service at the Methodist Church: ten A.M. From the street I hear the opening hymn.

Ericson's Methodist Episcopal Church was founded in 1884, but the current church was not built until the 1920s. It is a simple frame building painted white with a central peaked roof and four arched stained-glass windows running along each side of the sanctuary. I slip into a pew at the back of the church. Only the first three rows are filled, mostly with elderly parishioners. Perhaps five or six children dot the crowd.

The bulletin shows that the Reverend Coates preaches three sermons each Sunday at separate parishes in the hills: Greeley, Ericson, and Bartlett. The morning rolls along with prayers and Scripture readings, responses and organ music. I watch the crowd—ranchers with starched shirts buttoned high, bare heads, and hair greased into position, women in floral dresses, attentive to the words of the minister.

During a moment of community sharing, a woman in the congregation raises her voice to gain attention, then turns to me and points. The entire congregation shifts in their seats to stare as she introduces me and runs down a history of my family. She is delighted with my presence as a guest in their church. The minister welcomes me; the congregation gets an eyeful and nods. I feel as if I am on *Candid Camera*, and it is not a pleasant feeling. The "Unison Prayer" read from the bulletin caps my agitation: "Eternal God, forgive us for wasting the time you have given us. It is not that we are idle, but we are so often busy with the wrong things. . . . Our hours are filled, but our souls are often empty. Forgive us & change us. Help us to commit ourselves to more enduring values that we may make the most of the time we have, which you have given to

us out of your love. Amen." I slip out the back during the bene-
diction, before the swarms of friendly Methodists can engulf me.

Somehow my plans to visit Ericson's Catholic church, St. Teresa's, never come to fruition. Instead, I strike a different course,
spending the majority of my time in the hills in the saloons and
bars with the cowboys.

Outside the town of Ericson, north and west a few miles up the
River Road, lies the Pitzer Ranch, famous around the world for the
quarter horses bred there. Howard Pitzer, his wife, Florence, and
their daughter, Kay, came to Ericson in the 1940s. In the 1960s
Howard made his reputation on a horse named Two Eyed Jack.
Over the years people have come from all over the country, from
Canada, South America, and Australia to buy horses at the Pitzer
Ranch.

Even though I do not know the shape of the emerging narrative
I will write, my journalistic training demands that I interview these
people. I call the ranch and explain my mission; Howard's grand-
daughter, Jane Brinkman, eagerly offers to give me a tour.

The day I arrive is a sunny early summer afternoon. Jane walks
directly from the office to greet my car. She takes me into the tack
shop, trophy room, and office and introduces me to everyone, then
leads me behind the scenes through the complex of barns and corrals, joking with grooms and fielding bawdy comments from cowhands. She laughs and tosses her head, reaches for the handle of a
large door, and rolls it open to reveal the expansive interior of the
sale barn where Pitzer horse auctions are held. It is bigger than the
Ericson Livestock Commission arena. She shows me the grooming
area and rows of stables. We pass horses being washed, brushed,
and trimmed.

We tromp behind the main house to another set of older barns
and visit Two Eyed Jack, a chestnut-colored quarterhorse still beautiful at twenty-three years. Jane chatters lightly and continuously
about Pitzer lore. "He's out of commission now," she says, rubbing
Jack's forehead. He munches feed. "But we love him!" she bubbles,
and turns, motioning for me to follow. Two sons stand stud on the

ranch. She tells me their names and I forget them, following in her shadow around the last of the barns. She is gesturing, chatting with workers as she strolls the grounds, then walks toward her car.

"Come on," she calls. "I'll show you the North Ranch," a move I soon realize is a bad decision. Jane drives one of those aerodynamically designed cars that soar around corners, and she drives at breakneck speed up the River Road, swooshing around the bends, leaving my stomach halfway out in some pasture. I soon become dizzy, and work desperately to keep from vomiting with each curve in the road. She keeps up a steady patter of myth and story about the Pitzer dynasty. I grunt often, never letting on that I am so dizzy I can't even get a bead on the horizon. The rest of the afternoon is a blur. I do not know why I don't speak up and say I am sick. It is a time in my life, though, when speaking up for anything is hard.

Finally comes the end of the journey. Jane drops me off at the main ranch, where my car is parked outside the huge metal auction building. We shake hands, and I drive straight into Ericson and to the Hungry Horse, getting my bearings easily as the master of my own car. It has been weeks since I have graced the door of the Hungry Horse in the late afternoon. Inside, I see several people I know, and it feels like a homecoming.

Later Jane shows up, creating quite a flutter in the bar. She is not a striking girl, but she is single, of marrying age, and heir to a tiny horse kingdom. Cowboys crowd around, even though I hear she is engaged to a rancher from out west in the state. Conversation ripples the air, and Jane laughs often. She is full of goodwill and a kind of self-assurance I find unnerving.

I ride the horse that night. I don't remember how I get back to the Big Six.

Lean. Not quite desert, yet no oasis either. Earthen shades of brown, the green of grass, the yellow of prickly-pear flower, the bright purple of penstemon. Daisies.

When I stand in ungrazed prairie, looking all around, it appears that chaos reigns. Dozens of different grasses, forbs, and shrubs crowd the ground. I'm mid-dune right now, halfway up a slope. The dune tumbles down to a wet meadow and I see other species there, unlike those that brush my legs. Turning, studying the top of the dune, I see that another set of plants dominates there.

To the untrained eye this appears a riotous explosion of unruly weeds, spidering out across land with no direction, and yet with a closer look, what on the surface appears to have no guiding principle reveals itself as a highly ordered ecosystem, unfolding with quiet precision: in upland areas and on the tops of dunes, soapweed, little bluestem, prairie sandreed, June grass, needle-and-thread, switchgrass, and grama grow, favoring the dry, arid knolls. Water moves swiftly through the sandy soil. Only those plants with deep roots can make a home on these windy slopes.

Farther down the hill, different zones of vegetation occupy the dune, depending on water availability, soil composition, the direction and angle of slope. Some plant communities are stable over long periods of time; others, in areas disturbed by wind or overgrazing, where the roots of plants have been damaged, show yearly changes as longer-lived plants succeed short-lived pioneer species.

In the interdunal areas, where the water table is high, hay meadows, wet meadows, and marshes flourish with their own set of grasses and sedges, ferns and pondweeds, all adapted to a unique set of variables: soil quality, water supply, alkalinity, temperature, depth.

The value of close inspection reveals itself: Out of chaos emerges the rhythm of a pattern.

$\mathcal{M}$AD

DOG

Sometime during the next week I drive to Ord, seat of Valley County, thirty miles south and west of Ericson, to buy lettuce, apples, breakfast cereal, and bread at the Jack and Jill grocery store, and to select a crispie from the glass case at the bakery, a sweet swirl of dough topped with sugar that evokes memories of similar journeys years before with my mother. How that all led to a tavern called the Someplace Else and a man they called Mad Dog I'll try to tell.

I was cash poor in those days, had little need for money. Regularly my father traveled from Osceola to the Big Six bringing brown grocery sacks stuffed full of food. I was not responsible for utility bills, and there was no rent to pay. A grant from the university had covered the cost of film and supplies. Still, I wanted money in my pocket, and when I emerged from the Jack and Jill grocery store and bumped into an employment agency next door, I was unable to control the desire to march in and apply for a job. Now, I could say I forgot about my master's project, but that would be untrue. Instead, I should say yellow sun soaked it out of me; ripe wind blew all direction from me. I should say the cicadas' voices called to me from the elms on Ord's town square, and like sirens, they lured me from the path.

I pushed open the door of the Ord employment agency, greeted the lone clerk, and listed my vital statistics on a three-by-five card. The pale gentleman filed my life in a small metal box on the top of his desk. I don't recall our conversation or the details of my entry. I do remember searching my past for pertinent experience. Years before, I had fled college with a girlfriend and moved for adventure across the country to Cape Cod. Eventually we both ended up in the lucrative restaurant business as waitresses, and while I had always hated the detail work of waiting tables— "Ketchup, please! Waitress, I wanted this steak cooked medium. Could you bring some more crackers? I need a Coke"—I was especially adept at hustling drinks, memorizing regulars' needs, and keeping up the patter of party conversation. On the card I wrote, "Position seeking: cocktail waitress," knowing in some mental chamber that in Ord, Nebraska, that was a long shot. I thanked the gentleman and walked into the midday glare of downtown Ord. The smell of freshly baked doughnuts floated on air from the bakery. I slid into the seat of my AMC, unwrapped my crispie, and drove north into the hills, promptly forgetting my actions.

Within a week the call came. A man at the end of the line identified himself as Pete from the Someplace Else. "When would you be available for an interview?" he asked.

I hesitated.

"Wednesday?"

It took a moment to realize my job application was being pursued. "Late morning," I blurted.

"Good. Eleven o'clock. We're on the south side of the square."

Days later I drove to Ord. A few doors west of the Jack and Jill, a blinking neon sign jutted from the block of storefronts: "Someplace Else." The doorway was set in an alcove with an air conditioner roaring and dripping above the frame. Inside, a long, narrow room stretched into shadows. The floor was plank wood, the ceiling high, perhaps twenty feet, with what appeared to be original pressed tin. A row of booths lined the west wall to my right. On the left was a walk-in cooler that stretched the length of the twenty-foot bar. Metal stools lined the counter. Far in the back I could make out several old-fashioned metal kitchen tables with straight-back chairs and a group of pool tables even farther beyond, toward the rear of the cavernous establishment.

The room was quiet, and only one customer slumped at the bar over a glass of beer. A man with silvery gray hair and wire-rimmed glasses stepped from behind the bar and offered his hand.

"Hi, I'm Pete." He was dressed in a pearl-snap cowboy shirt and jeans.

"Lisa Norton," I said, extending my hand, smiling, trying to look both angelic and seasoned at the same time. He led me to a booth and asked if I'd like something to drink. I opted for a Coke, and he brought a basket of popcorn.

We talked for several minutes. He was inquisitive but not pushy, the kind of man I wouldn't mind chatting with over a cold beer in a bar sometime. I noticed his eyes were blue and watery behind his glasses.

"When can you start?" he asked.

I had the immediate sensation of waking up on a train leaving a station and realizing it was the wrong train. In those years, though, I had no skills to call to the conductor, "Wait! Wait!," no ability to stop a situation careening out of control. I remained polite and settled in for my ride.

"This weekend?" I offered.

"Fine. You come on over tomorrow at five and we'll get you set up."

It was done. I rose and turned for the door. The view beyond the picture windows—tawny-colored marble courthouse, lush American elms, sunlight filtered onto grass—would soon become familiar.

Back at the Big Six I skimmed a box of books packed in from the University of Iowa. I have vague memories of titles about communication theory and the history of the press. They were collecting dust. It was clear even then that I would not read those books that summer. I should have packed them up and shipped them back. That would have been an honest acknowledgment of my shifting priorities, but back then I didn't recognize a shift, because I didn't know how to go into the hills and get a story in the first place. So I kept the dry academic tracts, and I kept wandering forward, watching for signs.

When news rippled through the family about my employment, my mother wondered why I hadn't taken a job at the Hungry Horse, which was, she said, the focus of my investigation. It was a good question and one I was unable to answer. I had some sense that the Hungry Horse was simply too close to the source, to a past I was still reluctant to investigate. Perhaps I preferred to keep it an idyllic cowboy bar in my mind and not cloud my images with the inevitable insider arguments that arise at any place of employment. Perhaps I was scared of working in a town that had for all my life been a fantastic landscape, an escape world distanced from day-to-day reality. Or perhaps I simply needed the anonymity of a different town and an out-of-the-way bar with an improbable name to see my way into the future.

That first night Pete showed me around the place. He set me up with a drink tray and a bank, as he called it. I was responsible for making change for drinks and snacks throughout the evening. I was in charge of the popcorn, and Pete directed me to the Red Baron pizzas, the highlight of our menu. I remember feeling awkward and out of place as the regulars arrived, eyeing me as if I were some mystifying piece of artwork invading their known and comfortable world. Somehow I made it through the evening, wiped the tables, swept the floor, and washed the glasses. At two A.M. I set out across darkened prairie shielded by a sky bigger than land, washed with white like a river in spring. Stars blurred into galaxies, and I felt like a piece of something large, rotating to its own rhythm.

For the next few weeks I drove to Ord every Thursday, Friday, and Saturday, late in the wind-driven summer afternoons, sometimes wearing shorts and a T-shirt. I parked on the north side of the square and carried my clothes up the marble steps and down into the basement of the solid stone courthouse. It was cool inside the wooden stall in the women's rest room, and there in the dim yellow light of a lone bulb I squeezed into my Levi's, slipped a cotton blouse over my head, and ran a brush through my hair. Perspiration gathered between my breasts. A small drop snaked its way down my belly and into the hollow of my navel. I walked out into the breathless Nebraska summer, across the courthouse lawn, through the soft shade of the elms and into the world called Some-place Else.

One night I wore a spaghetti-strap sundress to work and my strap broke. Pete slipped a small, neatly wrapped pack from his wallet. Inside was one needle and some white thread.

"Comes in real handy," he says, smiling in a fatherly way. With great decorum he stitches the strap to the dress. We stand motion-less outside the door of the big walk-in cooler. I feel vulnerable, but Pete is all gentleman. He tells me about similar moments in his life, and while I hold my breath he puts me back together again, then sends me onto the floor to take care of our patrons.

That night the Bohemians arrive. Throughout Nebraska there are descendants of Czech immigrants who came to this region in the late 1800s. We Nebraskans affectionately call them Bohemians. Tonight they straggle in off the street like a parade of clowns—first father, then mother, followed by a clump of noisy children, trailed by brothers and sisters-in-law, more children, then a grand-mother or two, all scrubbed and combed for a night on the town, the men dressed in jeans and T-shirts, the women in cotton slacks and blouses, the children in shorts, sleeveless shirts, and miniature cowboy boots or Keds. They take up residence at the steel, lino-leum-covered kitchen tables. Immediately Father turns in his chair and hails me with a foreign phrase I do not understand. The body language I recognize, and I hustle over.

He wants to inspect my dress first; he tells me I look like I'm wearing a wedding dress. I wonder what kind of weddings he's been to. He turns to the others at the table and fires off a few Czech lines. They look at me and laugh. He orders drinks for the table, and I turn for the bar, swearing under my breath.

The Bohemians are loud and they sit sideways on their chairs, waiting for me to come within earshot, when they call out for more beer. The children drop quarters in the jukebox and the walls reverberate with accordion-backed polkas. Father wants to dance and he swings and stomps with his wife around the pool table. He is a square, short man with black hair and heavy-framed glasses. He wears a clean white T-shirt and cerulean Lee slacks, the kind they only sell in small-town western-wear shops across the Great Plains and the agricultural belt of this country. They're for workingmen— farmers and ranchers—who like to go to town weekend nights but don't want to wear their Sunday best. Mother has wispy brown hair, like a halo around her angelic face. Her skin is pink and plump, unlined by sun. I imagine she cooks all day, for family and for church. She has full, round hips, and her brown slacks hug her figure. She wears a hand-sewn cotton blouse printed with a tiny daisy pattern. It is buttoned high around her neck. They dance like young lovers; he cradles and guides her ripe, soft form around the cavernous interior of the Someplace Else, dodging chairs and tables in their private yet formal dance of abandon.

As the evening rolls into darkness, the conversation at the Bohemians' tables slips into a broken half-Czech, half-English, and they order drinks in this barely decipherable tongue. They take great pleasure in my mistakes and make sure the whole place knows if I have erred when I arrive balancing a tray of bottles and glasses and an armload of popcorn in baskets.

Weekly I dread their arrival and await their departure with mixed yearning and dismay. They have never learned the art of tipping, and they leave behind a quarter or two—almost as if it were a mistake—for my full evening of service.

Somewhere in here the Fourth of July happens, a holiday laden with emotion from my past, a time of family and early birthday celebrations, of remarkably similar sun-soaked summer days stretching over years of memory, of afternoons spent in the company of my cousin Miles, of play in water, of safety in known family patterns. It has been years since I have spent a Fourth at the Big Six, and this one quickly becomes impossible for me to deal with. My father is remarried; my cousin is absent. I spend the day at the Hungry Horse, where things feel familiar. I am surrounded by friends, many of them from the old days, and we drink our way toward the afternoon, tipping long-neck bottles of Bud and Miller, flirting and pumping the jukebox for wailing tunes by Willie Nelson and Crystal Gayle.

Outside on Ericson's wide dusty street the annual noon Fourth of July parade marches from the west end of town into the shade of the huge cottonwoods at the east end. Horsemen carrying flags lead the parade. First there's the Stars and Stripes, then the American Legion banner and the blue-and-yellow Great Seal of the State of Nebraska fluttering in a limp breeze. Children on bikes and miniature three-wheeled roadsters follow. An odd assortment of kids and adults walk behind, some dressed in Old West gear, the others in leftover pieces of what appear to be once-cherished Halloween or school play costumes. Anyone can join the parade, and some walk along the edges of the ragtag procession in street clothes, tossing handfuls of Brach's candy to the children, friends hailing and waving, kids massing at their feet.

Next come the quarter horses, groomed to perfection and mounted by proud teens and seasoned old-timers with creased and sweat-stained Stetsons. Then the floats, sponsored by 4-H, the Hungry Horse Saloon, the Methodist and Catholic church women, and perhaps a class from the consolidated high school in Bartlett, the county seat and only other town in Wheeler County. A few old wagons are drawn by a few old plow horses. The tiny high school band high-steps in time with the lone drummer, stopping once or twice during the length of Ericson's one business block to play Sousa tunes and finally the national anthem, when all stand, grown men slapping their hands across their hearts and warbling into the hot, flat, white light of Ericson, midday.

Residents and lake folks line the sidewalks, sitting in lawn chairs or leaning against the façade of the Ericson Locker, resting on the steps of the post office, or across the street sitting on the plank benches in front of Foster's Market, run by Mike and Blanche. Others slip into the shade of the covered boardwalk that fronts the

Hungry Horse, which dominates the south side of the street. The parade takes all of fifteen minutes, but it is a festive quarter hour of community spirit. Afterward, people wander back and forth across the street, visiting with neighbors and annual lake residents. Some cross the street to a church stand set up in the fire station which sells barbecued-beef sandwiches with a dollop of potato salad and a Dixie cup full of purple Kool-Aid. Then a good portion of the crowd piles into the Hungry Horse to jockey for stools around the bar and crowd the tables. Someone racks the balls on the pool table, and the jukebox belches forth the croon of another lonesome cowboy. Barefoot kids run in and out the open door. Scruffy dogs prowl outside for some master lost deep within the Saloon.

Others walk or caravan to the rodeo grounds west of Main Street, where there is a kids' rodeo and an adult tug-of-war with both female and male divisions. The rodeo stands afford no shade, and men in suspenders and seed-corn caps sit stoically with wives in sleeveless blouses to watch grandchildren rope calves, leap from working ponies, and wrestle yearlings to the ground, imitating older brothers and uncles who ride rodeo across the West.

But first, the tug-of-war competitions are staged. Men gear up by stripping off T-shirts and slugging back final gulps of soda pop. I'm accorded press status, because of my camera, although no one has spoken a word. I get right into the fray and shoot several images of sweaty cowhands digging boot heels into the dirt of the corral, faces pulled into tight masks of agonizing effort. Back and forth the rope shifts, and I jump from team to team, capturing the gripping hands, the slipping rope, the straining muscles. Afterward I wander the spectators and shoot images of little girls on big horses, of young cowboys-to-be, of farmers and ranchers, of brawny cowhands, but the sun is unrelenting, and I feel lightheaded from the breathless heat. After the first young cowhand shoots across the arena on his russet-colored pony, leaning forward, spinning his rope, I find myself back in the sheltering shade of the Hungry Horse with others of the drinking crowd. It is perhaps two P.M., and the day's festivities have only begun.

Later, after the evening fireworks, there will be a country-and-western band and a dance in the beer garden behind the Hungry

Horse. For now, though, the crowd dissipates. Lake residents drive back down the River Road to mow lawns and splash in the cool lake water. Many of the ranch families have packed up coolers of chicken and coleslaw and headed for friends' and relatives' houses to await the evening fireworks. The church women serve the last of the barbecue sandwiches, potato salad, and Kool-Aid, and business at the Hungry Horse moves into the midafternoon lull.

To tell the truth, I cannot remember what I did next. It would have been like me to drive back to the Big Six, change into a swimming suit, and hike up the Cedar to a swimming hole, but I don't recall if I chose this solitary path. As a kid I would have set out with Cousin Miles to play on the island or at the beach. My mother would have fed us sandwiches before we left, admonishing us to come in out of the sun soon, and we would have dashed off, towels flying like capes behind us, rubber thongs slapping at our feet. But that was a long time ago, and my mother is gone, and my cousin Miles is not here, and I am well past the era of afternoons played out in imaginary worlds of joint creation. By dusk, though, I am back at the Horse, where I pile into a pickup with a bunch of cowhand rowdies and drive to the lake for fireworks. Not far from where we park sits the dock of my childhood, thrusting into the north end of Lake Ericson in front of my uncle's cabin. Just yards away, on this day, for years, I dangled toes into cool water, oohing and aahing at the magic in the sky, resting sure that life was safe and predictable. I look across dark water to catch a glimpse of that girl, but she is not there. I drink another beer and bullshit with the boys.

Several people tend bar at the Someplace Else, and over the weeks I learn to work with each of them. Jack, who owns the bar with his wife, Eve, is all business when he mixes drinks. He is a man I remember as circular, rather than angular, like so many men in the hills. He has a soft belly and buzz-cut hair. He wears knit shirts with slacks and oxfords when he works. Jack moves quickly on his feet, and his all-work-no-play demeanor elicits my best good-girl behavior. Eve moves more slowly around the bar, careful of her long fingernails. She wears her auburn hair stacked high atop her head. She stares at me a lot. Finally she breaks down and asks, "Honey, do you ever wear makeup?"

"No," I tell her, trying to smile, "I never do."

Pete is Jack's brother and there are rumors about why he's working at the Someplace Else, stories about what he did before, but I like Pete and I protect him, and I only listen with one ear to the rumors. He is as exacting in his work as Jack, but he is easier to be around, more able to crack a smile and a joke, and I am always happy when Pete is tending bar. I know he will coach me if I bungle an order and remind me patiently to take popcorn if I've forgotten to scoop baskets and carry them to the table.

My favorite bartender, though, is Lydia. She is short and buxom and smart, and she helps me sort out my tangle of drinks and tabs with a precision and grace I admire.

"Let's see . . . I had three Windsor Cokes, a pitcher of Pabst, two Millers, one Bud, a vodka tonic, and a rum and Coke." I start scratching figures on a napkin.

"Fourteen twenty-five," she says, some mental calculator having tallied the numbers.

I am distracted by music and voices hollering for beer, and I suppose I gawk at her.

"A little trick I learned in school," she says, and we laugh. There is no arrogance in her skill.

"You'll get it," she says to me, conviction in her eyes.

I can tell she is a woman of untapped potential. She may be about my age, but our paths have been so different. She grew up near Ericson, has relatives there, finished high school, but did not have the opportunity of college. She married young, quickly had children. Her husband—well, he drinks a little too much, like so many in these hills, and I come to believe that she supports the family. I like her strength. We agree to get together for pizza later in the summer, but for now it's just a barrage of Windsor and Coke, Budweiser and pitchers of Pabst.

*   *   *

Mornings at the Big Six I wrap myself in a fluffy pink robe and carry a cup of coffee to the plank desk on the small side porch. Sun breaks through cottonwoods in the east, above switchgrass and frame cabins and rusting trailers. Leaves quiver. The scent of dew-soaked grass floats in air. I pull up a captain's chair and write long descriptions in my journal. Outside on the ground, robins teach their young to hunt for worms. A family of cottontails lives in the lilac bush at the corner of the cabin, and small bunnies hop out to feed on tender blades of grass growing in the southeast corner of the yard. I watch all this, hush-mouthed from my hidden observatory, calm in these moments, knowing that in this quiet activity rests the answer I seek. Still, I am unable to find my way into the story about the Sandhills I have said I will write. I do not know what to say or how to say it. Much later I find this entry in my journal:

"I feel like there is something—somewhere between heart and intellect—that is desperately wrong with me. Soul perhaps? Do I suffer an affliction of the soul?"

There is a young man who frequents the Someplace Else on weekends. He is younger than I by ten years or so, but he likes me; it is evident, and I am flattered. He comes in late, well after dark on Saturdays. He is scrub-faced and wind-burned. His sandy hair is cropped in a crew cut, but I only know this because he removes his hat once to run his hand across the top of his head. He fits the crown back like it is part of the skull, never to remove it again in my presence.

His eyes are clear, piercing blue, and he directs them at me when he thinks I am not looking, but he never speaks. He drinks whiskey. In his fresh button-down western shirt, his worn but clean jeans, and his buffed boots, he looks too young to drink whiskey. He looks as if he ought to be going to church with his mom, and I sense he is seeking a girl who can be like a mom, and I try to be kind to him, but he spooks easy, like a wild pony. All summer long he comes in, late, after ranch work and gazes at me.

I learn a little about him from the others, and I know his uncle from the Hungry Horse—a good-hearted man who drinks too much. One night late, driving back to Ericson from Ord, I pass a cowboy on the side of the road. I recognize his gait, and slow to give him a ride. It is the uncle. He can't remember where he parked his truck, so he is walking home. I give him a lift up the highway a couple miles to the ranch he shares with his nephew, the young tongue-tied one.

People say the uncle is hard on the boy, makes the kid carry more than his share of the responsibility for the ranch. I don't know about that, but I do know a little about the demons that haunt that young man's soul.

One night, late, I agree to follow him to his ranch; he has managed to find the words to say he wants to show it to me, so I go, mostly out of sympathy for the boy, so locked up inside himself. We tour the grounds and ranch house. He motions with his hands, like a mute struggling with sign language. I can tell he is bursting with things to say, but words seem foreign to his mouth. Ideas spin in his mind, but his lips simply cannot fit themselves around words. I hurt for him all tangled up in his heart, but I leave him there that night. I sense he wants more. He wants me to hold him, to rock him and tell him the world is a safe place, but I cannot, and when I walk away, I believe he sits with his head in his hands and cries.

Ed's a regular at the Someplace Else. He comes in every evening after work and settles onto the last stool at the bar, closest to the door. He orders a draw. The first time I refill it, I set his glass on the bar sink and reach for a new one.

"Nope," he says. "You use that same glass. Those new ones, they got soap film on them. Makes the beer flat. I just got that glass cleaned up."

I never know what Ed does for a living, but he wears the garb of a utility worker or auto mechanic. He is consistent and quiet and he stays on his stool for hours, drinking slowly, always from the first glass he is served.

There is a woman who often joins him. Clarrie. She is thin and pale and wears her waist-length brown hair straight, parted in the middle and combed slick to her head. She wears tight tank tops and jeans and smokes Marlboros, which she carries in a cigarette case that she sets on the counter in front of her, along with her keys, her wallet, and an ashtray. She drapes her jacket over the back of the stool and settles in for the evening. I get the sense that she and Ed are old friends, bar buddies. If Ed is absent she banters with Pete, but mostly she keeps to herself, smoking cigarette after cigarette and sipping a Windsor Coke.

She is friendly to me, but I do not get to know her, and no one speaks of her to me. I notice she is often absent from her chair for long periods, but I am busy and do not have time to dwell on her behavior. The next time I look, she is back.

Years later I learn she is a lady of the evening. I learn it in a backwards way, and it breaks my heart. I hear that two drifters have been doing construction work at the lake and the cops have made them pull up a concrete floor they have laid. Rumor has it a body may be under the floor, but it isn't. The body they seek is Clarrie's. Seems she left the Someplace Else one night, like so many nights— jacket draped over her chair, Marlboro smoking in the ashtray— but she never came back. Never. Local police think the two drifters killed her, but they never find any evidence and the drifters disappear from the County, and Clarrie is gone, forever, from the story of Ord, Nebraska, and the Someplace Else.

I meet Tom on a hot July night, with light bending around the buildings on the west side of the square. It is warm, angular, late-day sun, and it illuminates the courthouse lawn and benches like a stage spotlighted with yellow beams. He comes into the Someplace Else for a Coke, says he doesn't drink, and we visit. He is a big, burly, sad man—teddy-bear-like, thoughtful and wounded— one of the walking wounded, a friend who lived through Vietnam would say. He is not a threat, and I agree to meet him in the courthouse square the next evening.

It is well past five P.M. when we mount the marble stairs and lean our backs against the warm stone walls of the courthouse façade. Tom tells me tales of the years he spent deep-sea diving. He talks with passion of the work, the undersea world of water and fish, of moray eels and sharks.

"Why are you here?" I ask. It is a direct question and he dodges, spinning out a complicated story about illness caused by rising too swiftly from the depths. I don't understand, but I back away from probing questions, and we begin the dance of our friendship, both of us sensing the other is harboring secrets, both of us curious but respectful of the other's privacy, both of us protective of our own pain. We meet several times over the weeks, just to sit and talk. He never attempts to hustle me, and I know he will not. It is an unspoken understanding. We are friends, partial confidants, sounding boards for as much as we are able to share at that tentative time in our lives.

I learn he is originally from Lincoln, the state capital, and that he, like many of the men around town, is working on the massive dam project going on upriver from Burwell in Garfield County. A reservoir is being created on the Calamus River—for irrigation and recreation, as the officials put it. When I drive by to see the monstrosity later in the summer, I am appalled by the devastation done to the landscape, but the wider implications for the ecology of the area are a far-off concern for me.

Tom is sad about being landlocked, but something keeps him here. I never discover the source of that internal commitment. Instead we talk about the sea, about travel, about our dreams.

Somehow Larry finds his way into the Someplace Else, too, and I wish he hadn't. He sulks at Ed's end of the bar long after Ed has gone home. He wears a black leather jacket and his straight blond hair hangs over his collar. He reminds me of some filthy creature, like an ungroomed, rabid cat. He slumps at the far end of the counter and grins at me, a wide, lascivious grin. His sleepy blue eyes seem to laugh at me and undress me all at the same time, and I wish we could kick him out. It is my job to be polite to him, though, so I do my best to make him feel welcome in our establishment. I use my most formal behavior with him— polite but proper. Still, he leers at me nightly from his lone post at the end of the bar. He constantly asks me out. I repeatedly refuse.

He tells me he's been in the penitentiary, just got out—something to do with theft and guns. He skirts the details. I don't ask. He reports it all as if it were a recent glory trip around the world and I should be heralding his return, as if a parade should be staged in his honor, as if he is a gift to me and to the world. He makes me nervous in a way that is hard to describe and perhaps harder for those who have not lived through assault to understand.

In the first hours after I was attacked, in shock, lost, grappling for a hold on life, I remember feeling knocked down a peg, demeaned, as if I had been too prideful of myself, falsely full of who I was. What I internalized from that moment was simple: Should I get my pride up too high, someone would take a whack at me; someone would put me in my place. Larry resonated on a very deep level as the kind of guy who would gladly put me in my place, in a base and defiling way, and so I was scared of him, and although I kept my formal manner, I also felt that if I acted too uppity around him, he would hurt me. With him I was a conflicted character; my behavior was erratic. Hot/cold all in one gulp.

Certainly this entire period in my life was a conflicted time, a time when I did not understand who I was, where I was going, or what my actions implied. Those realities inevitably generated all sorts of mixed signals. It was as if I were wearing finely tuned radar, adjusted to keep me alive. My responses to that overly sensitive radar, though, were governed by an as yet unconstructed set of perceptions and values. I was still building a world to live in, a new world that could replace the one stripped from me four years earlier on a rainy night, in a city whose name I would like to forget.

Quite simply, Larry set off my alarm. His was the most basic kind of danger: life-threatening. My radar went wild around him, and my behavior wavered. When I was overly formal, I worried that he would decide to knock me down a peg, that he would be waiting for me after work. I started parking my car directly in front of the Someplace Else. Still, I thought, he could hide on his Harley in the shadows of the grain elevators north of town and follow me into the lonely, abandoned hills, force me off the road . . .

My mind ran with horrid details. Consequently, I fluctuated between off-putting formality and tentative friendliness, in hopes that I could keep him pacified, keep him from hurting me. I assumed this was all my responsibility. It was a very dark time in my life.

Today I would tell him, "Keep the hell away from me!" I would have Pete throw him out. I would alert the police if I had to. I would mobilize my cowhand friends at the Hungry Horse. I would carry a gun. But that is me today. Back then I was very confused about which and whose actions in the world were my responsibility—I was one of the walking wounded.

Sometime after the Fourth of July and before Ericson's Turtle Races in August, there was another man who came into the Someplace Else. I'll call him Parker. His friends called him Mad Dog.

The first time he came through the door is burned onto the screen of my mind. His frame fills the doorway. He is turned slightly to the right and his profile is in silhouette, his whole presence merely a shadow beyond the glass. Then he steps into the room, lightly, as if he is moving to a tune no one else hears. His face is broad, with a strong jaw. A red bandanna circles his blond, wind-blown hair. He is wearing a yellow T-shirt and jeans. His arms are solid and tan, his eyes wide-set and blue as summer sky. An infectious and slightly lopsided smile rides his lips, as if a punch line waits to be told. When he smiles, I see two rows of brilliant, straight white teeth. He straddles a stool, orders a Bud. We don't talk that night. Pete serves him. I am busy and I try to act as if he is just another customer. My skin, though, tells me he is not. I realize I am hoping he won't leave, but of course he does. Two Buds and he's out the door. I wait for him every night after that. I cannot help myself.

He begins coming in as a regular, and Pete takes to teasing me about that big blond guy.

"But there are others who come in, too," I remind Pete, unwilling to acknowledge the interest I must be wearing like a sign.

"Yeah, business's been great since we hired you."

I let his comment slide.

Weekly, when Parker comes in and takes his seat, we nod. I remain aware of his presence every minute he is there, although we do not talk, and I think it is Pete, finally, who drags me into a conversation with him.

It is instant camaraderie, like old friends being reunited. We have many issues to discuss, and we get right down to some ancient, unfinished conversation, not unlike my friendship with teddy-bear Tom, except this is different, very different. Being near Parker makes the hairs on my skin stand in alert little rows.

For several weeks he comes in each Thursday, Friday, and Saturday night. He stays only as long as he can engage me in conversation. When the crowd gets too rowdy, he heads back to his motel. He, too, is working on a construction project in the county and living out of a suitcase far from home.

"When are you going to go out with that good-looking guy?" Pete asks me after Parker leaves.

"Never. Someday. I don't know, Pete. We're friends."

"Ummm . . . he's a handsome man."

I suppose I blush and give myself away.

In time Parker asks me out. I invite him to visit me at the Big Six and give him directions. I remember dressing in the soft light of evening, jittery, like a teenage girl on her first date. I hear his motorcycle long before I see him clear the row of cedars along the road in the west. The cycle makes a wide, soft turn into the yard of the Big Six. I don't even recall inviting him in, although I must have. Did we go for a drink at the Hungry Horse? I don't think so. I only recall flashes of scenes from that evening: I see us under the big round wooden roof of the old merry-go-round. We must have walked around the lake, me pointing to places in the landscape and telling the stories. We stopped at the pavilion, now converted to a picnic shelter, and sat side by side on a table. It was dark and fireflies were our only light. I remember wanting his touch, craving the feel of his lips, but we were like children, tentative and unsure. We flirted and joked. I watched Derald's pickup creep past along the north and east sides of the pavilion and I could tell he and Jewel were watching us.

Later they told me they were cheering inside the cab: "Kiss her! Kiss him!"

Instead, we watched the lake and Parker told me about his childhood in Nebraska. I told him about my studies at the University. Mosquitoes buzzed our heads, arms, and legs, and we slapped and scratched, laughing at our vulnerability to these tiny pests and at our relative indifference, our determination to sit in the dark under a teetering pavilion in the swampy cedar smell of a quiet Sandhills lake, late on a night in the warm, expectant month of July, alone, yet together, in a place that seemed abandoned by all but the creatures of the night.

We walked west along the sandy road back to the Big Six. Parker took my hand. It was a sweet gesture, and I held his like a schoolgirl. At the cabin he grasped the handlebars of his cycle, kicked up the stand, and swung his leg over the seat. He steadied the bike between his legs and in one smooth, rounded movement reached out for me and folded me into his body. As I moved into him and the warmth of our bodies mingled, I felt at once home.

We fell in easily with each other—no pretensions, no games. In time I met his friends. They assured me he had an angry temper— Mad Dog, they'd nicknamed him—but oddly, I never saw it.

One Saturday night at the Someplace Else, the Bohemians gave a peak performance, cracking jokes about my clothes and service and mentioning repeatedly their band and next gig Sunday afternoon. Father and some of his cousins, brothers, or buddies had formed a polka band, and they would be playing at the local drinking establishment in the fading frontier town of Comstock, south and west of Ord in Custer County. Parker suggested we ride to Comstock the next day and drop in on the Bohemians. I thought he was daft.

"I gave my best Saturday-night energy to those thankless guests. Why would I want to spend Sunday with them?"

"You'll see," he said, a playful smile touching his lips.

The next day Parker rolled into the yard of the Big Six just after the noon whistle blasted the clear Ericson air.

"Come on," he called through the open window. "Let's drive to Comstock."

I bounded out the back door. "You're serious?"

"Let's go."

I slipped a pack over my shoulders and swung my bare leg over the motorcycle, settling into the seat and wrapping my body into Parker's.

We rolled out of the yard, onto the River Road, into Ericson and out of town on Highway 91. Seven miles west we cut south on Highway 70, barreling through high blue skies and prairie dunes waving with grass and sunflowers. We didn't talk, just cruised, our bodies leaning with the road.

In Ord we stopped at a café, ate lunch, then drove west on gravel. Back roads in the Sandhills shoot straight over the horizon, seemingly in pursuit of something, and yet once the highest dune is reached, nothing materializes, just more sand and hills. Perhaps cattle graze. Perhaps a lone Siberian elm or cottonwood hugs a ditch, but for the most part the land is wide open, fence lines the only mark of man.

In about half an hour we approached the cottonwoods of Comstock. They were visible from miles away, and I knew a small part of what early settlers must have felt when they approached a prairie town, could see it glimmer on the horizon, far out from the buckboard, or from the wagon rut they walked, how it must have made their mouth water just a bit, brought lightness to their step.

The tavern was on the south side of Comstock's one long street. Right across on the north side was Wescott, Gibbons and Bragg's Store, a building I'd read about, listed on the National Register of Historic Places, and moved across the Middle Loup River from the budding town of Wescott in 1900. Comstock was thriving then as a newly established railroad town, and Wescott, Gibbons and Bragg's Store did a swift business as one of the only trading centers in the Sandhills.

We parked the cycle and I walked across the deserted street. Inside the smudged windows I could see old equipment and a jumble of boxes. The store was long closed and the town was well past its prime. Outside on the front of the building hung the original drugstore sign:

DRINK

COCA-COLA

DELICIOUS AND REFRESHING

Parker was standing on the curb in front of Bud's & Vic's Lounge. His hair was tousled, slipping out of the bandanna that crossed his forehead. Accordion music seeped through the screen door and into the street. "This is the place," he said.

Inside, my eyes struggled to make out the details. A small band crowded a raised platform at the back of the room, but I couldn't make out the faces. My ears picked up drums, an accordion, and an electric bass. I heard Father call out to us just as the band launched into a rousing polka tune. We sat at a small round table. A woman walked over from the bar.

"What'll it be?"

"Couple of Buds."

A few people hunched at the bar on stools; others were scattered among the round tables in front of the band. Long-neck bottles of Miller and Bud dripped sweat. Several couples moved to the dance floor and began stomping around the room. Father was delighted to see us; he smiled broadly as his arms pumped the accordion and his fingers worked the keys. Looking around, I began to recognize some of the patrons. Mother sat at a table with one of her sisters, cousins, or in-laws; it was hard to know the pedigree. Two of the children who came to the Someplace Else with their parents sipped clear liquid through straws from stubby bar glasses. Polkas, then waltzes filled the air, one after the other. We ordered another round, watched the dancers swinging partners, and tapped our feet. As we downed our second beer, the band took a break. We smiled idiotically in the direction of the Bohemians.

"Great music!" I yelled. Father merely dipped his shoulders and did a little hangdog chin act. Mother smiled at us for him. We took this as our cue, left a tip on the table, and moved for the door, turning to wave and call thanks.

In the street I burst into laughter, more perhaps at my presence in this setting than at the scene itself.

Parker just smiled. "They're good people," he said.

"Oh, don't be so damn serious. It was a hoot."

"What, you don't like polka?"

I should have known by the look in his eyes that I was in for it, but he had scooped me into his arms and was leading me into a rollicking polka right there on Comstock's abandoned Main Street, before I could turn and run. We stomped up a cloud of dirt, then couldn't contain ourselves and dissolved into laughter, our feet getting all tangled up. It was midafternoon and a breeze had finally begun to stir the leaves of the cottonwoods. Parker kicked the cycle into action; I climbed on behind him and we rode east down the broad, shaded road and back into the sun-blasted hills.

Weekly Parker drove to the Big Six and we grilled burgers on the porch, then sat in evening sun and talked. I wish I could remember the specifics of our conversations, but I cannot. I do remember, though, feeling completely at ease with Parker. He was a sensitive soul beneath his rough exterior, and in me he found a listening ear. It was during this period that the dreams started to haunt my nights. I remember waking once in a panic. I had dreamed a horrible murder had taken place inside the Big Six. The scene still emblazoned in my memory is opening the door to the back porch and seeing blood everywhere. Body parts had been flung around the room. I woke up breathing hard. Parker held me while I cried, purring soft words. Had I told him the details of my past? Had I told him I had almost been murdered on a dark city street, a crazed scream strangled in my throat? I do not know. Instead, I recall simply lying in the arms of this good man and weeping—for the fear evoked by the ghastly dream, for the loss of innocence, for the loss of stability, for the loss of everything I had been.

In the morning we never spoke of it; we just moved on. But the dreams did not stop coming: dogs hungry for blood chasing me, running, running, running, and always that dog at my heels. Dogs— rabid, vicious dogs—locked in rooms into which I was thrown. No windows. No escape. I slept fitfully, always crawling into the comforting arms of Parker if he was there, or calling to hear his voice if he was not. I was very alone, even when I was surrounded by life.

During the day I took a beach towel and wandered the sandy road to an abandoned dock at the north end of the lake. I eased down the weather-bent, rickety stair steps, spread my towel on the dock, inches above water, and soaked up sun for an hour, a slight breeze lapping at my toes, pushing hair across my forehead. Dragonflies buzzed the willow bushes along the banks, hovered above my legs. Bluegills in the water below the planks moved languidly through shallow warm water.

It was during these daily hours of sun and privacy that I imagined a life I could live in the future: I would be a writer, live in a cottage by the sea—No! I would be a writer and live in Ericson, looking across the lake into lonely windswept hills.

I drifted and dreamed and conjured water memories from my past: the sepia-toned color of the lake from under water, shot through with the yellow of sun's rays; the artesian well at Melville's dock, spilling blue water all day long; the spring below cedars that Billy found, buried beneath debris, how he took me there and we burrowed under low-hanging branches, how he pushed aside leaves and let me touch the cool water seeping from earth.

Early in August delivery trucks begin arriving in Ericson at the heady rate of two a day. From across the street at Mike Foster's Market I watch a man unload case after case of Budweiser and wheel it into the Hungry Horse. I wander over to get the scoop from Stan.

"Putting the final touches on the Turtle Races," he says. He tells me he's been at it since May, running ads and locating a band. "I ordered fifty extra cases of Bud."

"Yeah, I saw that from over at Mike's." I slide onto the stool next to the newspapers. Stan describes the beer garden and the band, Cactus Jack. I ask about his wife and order a cup of coffee. I learn the Sandhill Turtle Races began in 1975, when George Woodward owned the Hungry Horse. Some guy from Spalding walked in, set a turtle on the pool table, and bet everyone in the house he had the fastest turtle there. As the story goes, people were showing up with challengers within days. I'm apt to believe the local lore; it sounds exactly like the sort of prank that would spark imaginations at the Hungry Horse. The Turtle Races were launched that August to much hoopla: Woodward sold Henny Penny Chicken on Ericson's main street and somehow got hold of a five-hundred-and-eighty-two-pound Galápagos tortoise named Big Gussie, who presided over the event from her cage on Main Street.

"Two hundred and eighty-eight turtles are registered this year," Stan says. "That's forty-seven more than last year." He tells me he catches turtles to rent. So far he has thirty-four. "Another guy, he caught ninety-five, and all are rented. Fifty cents each." Stan squirts some 7-Up into a bar glass and sets his foot on a low shelf behind the counter. "Got a call the other day from New York City. Some guy wanted to rent a turtle and hire somebody to race it." He laughs. "Town board ordered a load of cinders. Filled up those potholes on Main Street."

"I didn't notice. I'll take a look on my way home." I feel chagrined that I have been oblivious to the flurry of preparation. I finish my coffee, decline a second refill, wish Stan a good day, and walk to my car. On Main Street I wave away a couple of flies buzzing my head, look west down the wide, sandy street toward the abandoned Purina Feed Store, across to the Ericson State Bank, the filling station, then up the block past Foster's Market and the fire station. No activity. I drive off in search of cinders.

By Saturday, Ericson's Main Street is parked solid with Ford pickups, El Dorados, and campers. I check license plates as I leave town for work in Ord: Nebraska, Iowa, Colorado, and Kansas.

At the Someplace Else the Bohemians straggle in for their weekly night on the town. They smile. I hurry to their table.

"I sure enjoyed your music the other day. You all want your usual?"

Father nods.

I ask if they've been playing long.

"Yep," he says.

"Well, I enjoyed myself. Thanks for inviting me." I turn toward the bar.

"We're there every Sunday," Father calls after me, his teeth glowing in his weather-burnt face.

"Great, that's real good. . . ."

Lydia has the pitcher filled before I even get to my station. I load the tray, scoop two baskets of popcorn, and carry everything to the table. Father pays without one comment on my outfit or service.

Sunday afternoon. About a hundred people gather at the softball diamond north of Ericson along Highway 91. A big white circle is chalked on the ground in the middle of the diamond, and two tables have been trucked in and set up near the circle. Bob Spilinek is at the microphone in the official role of announcer, and four locals sit behind the tables as judges. Two timers pace the circle, testing stopwatches. A boundary rope parallels the periphery of the circle.

I listen as the rules are read: "No lead ropes, no probes, and no mechanical devices are permitted. We expect that the natural ability of these turtles has not been hampered, nor heeded by the sharpening of claws or grease on the bottom of the shell. And absolutely no starting blocks."

A hush falls over the crowd. "Let the races begin," Bob's voice booms over the PA system.

A cardboard box is lifted from the center of the circle to reveal the first turtles, who seem stunned by the light and pull their heads in. The crowd stares at the shells and begins cheering as if they are watching the Kentucky Derby.

I walk over to the table to clarify the details. Jake Conner, one of the judges, tells me there are five classes of turtles: painted turtles, sand turtles, snappers, mud turtles, and leatherbacks.

The noise behind us peaks. We turn just as the first turtle makes it to the chalked finish line, crosses, and wins. A guy on the edge of the circle is leaning in on the boundary rope and shaking his fist in the air.

"So what's your strategy?" I call.

"Keep them on ice," he calls back.

His encampment is surrounded by coolers.

I catch sight of Parker's El Camino under the elms, walk over, slide into the seat, and kiss him as generously as possible. "It is so hot."

He steps out and reaches into the truck bed. I hear a lid creak. His hand comes back displaying two cold beers.

"Ummm . . . just what I needed. Thank you." I join him in the shade outside, and we pop the tabs. I drink a long, necessary gulp. The spectator stands are full of men and women, and the edges of the racing circle are surrounded by fidgeting children. Cars and trucks surround the area, with a wider circle of people resting on tailgates and lounging in lawn chairs. There isn't a cloud in the sky, not a touch of wind, and the sun is directly above us, beating down relentlessly. We stand away from the activity and drink.

"I've got to take some pictures. I'll be back." Over my shoulder I see Parker retreat for the El Camino. He leaves the door open and sits sideways on the seat, watching the crowd.

I snap images of victorious winners and turtles that haven't budged, their neck and legs retracted in disgust. There are turtle owners scolding their turtles like children and others praising turtles pawing along behind them on a leash.

Bob's voice cuts the air: "No drugged or artificially stimulated turtles will be allowed to race, and any found under the influence will be disqualified." A titter runs through the slightly inebriated crowd.

Finally the day's heat wears into late afternoon. Thunderclouds mass on the western horizon. "First you roast to death and then you drown." It's Jake. He droops in a chair behind the judges' table. He offers me his flask.

"Thanks, Jake." I take a sip. Whiskey.

"Here comes the rain!" Jake stands.

A wall of gray is moving toward the Turtle Races. St. Teresa's Catholic church across the road is in rain. The wall reaches the edge of the field, and the crowd hurries to fold chairs and stow tarps. Jake gathers some papers, shoves them inside his shirt, reaches under the table, and releases the leg lock. Engines purr and a line of vehicles parades toward the Hungry Horse.

I stand in the rain for a while, letting it soak my T-shirt and shorts. I feel like a piece of dried fruit, reconstituting. Parker waits in the car. "Let's hit the Horse," I say, sliding in beside him, and he joins the caravan to the bar.

The lot behind the Hungry Horse has been fenced and filled with picnic tables. Benches—wooden planks balanced on cinder blocks—line the fences. A bar has been set up near the back door of the saloon, and behind it sits a ten-foot horse tank crammed with fifty pounds of ice and bottle after bottle of beer. Parker and I quickly lose each other in the crowd, which is huge. Sometime during the evening, Stan bellows above the band that the crowd is near seven hundred. I record that fact in a small notebook, along with a variety of other snippets, most of which make no sense in the light of day.

The next morning I drive into town. Dee Foster catches the sun from the bench outside Foster's Market. A stray dog wanders Main Street. The Hungry Horse Saloon is empty, except for the regulars who flank the bar on stools. They conjure moments from the night before, replay them, and laugh.

"Hair of the dog . . . ?" that handsome cowboy calls to me.

I accept the offer and pull up a stool next to Rick Thorman. "This here's the most round-buying bar I ever been in," he says.

"I'll drink to that." Max raises his glass.

"Really!" Rick is emphatic. "You get down to that old Omaha

town and you don't have a roll of money in your butt pocket, you can sit there till you turn blue 'fore somebody buys you a drink."

"Here, here!" We all raise glasses to the Horse.

After that I hole up in the Big Six for three days to recover and ponder what I've witnessed. All I can remember I record in a notebook.

At this point, my notes and journal entries peter out. I have no event to hang my memories on, no letter or journal entry to help me organize the time. I know I continued to work at the Someplace Else, to spend time with Parker, to soak up healing sun, to frequent the Hungry Horse, and I know that cowboy continued to court me, despite my attachment to Parker and despite the cowboy's girlfriend at home. Still, how each day followed the other, what I felt in the ticking moments of wind and cottonwood rustle, what I dreamed, what I worried—all is part of a great gray stroke across my life.

Sometime in late August, I quit my job at the Someplace Else. I recall a growing weight of guilt over my uncompleted project. I felt I needed to focus on Ericson and the Hungry Horse, to do more research, to somehow ferret out more history, new statistics—something that would make the pieces of a story evident to me.

I drove frequently to Kearney, where Parker worked. He lived with a buddy, and while they went off to jobs during the day, I wandered the shops and bookstores of lazy downtown Kearney, a college town gripped by late-summer slumber. The western architecture of the city buildings, the promise of the impending school year, the people on the streets, the pickups they drove all reminded me of childhood and the landscape of another Nebraska town. This was the first time since the early 1970s that I had been present in Nebraska as summer closed and fall set in, and the angle of the light evoked a sense of homecoming I savored. I bought a cobalt-blue wool coat in preparation for winter, and a blank book in which to write.

On weekends Parker and I drove to small towns in Buffalo and Custer counties to visit with his parents and his brothers and their families. Their lives were settled and domestic. I could tell that was what Parker wanted, too. During the week, in the evening, we rode his motorcycle to the Derby to drink, or out into country west of Kearney to Parker's friends' house, Sally and Dean's, where there was always a party. While the guys played cards, Sally and I visited, listened to music, and drank beer. It was always the same gang, many of whom I liked, but in time I began to feel itchy inside, as if my soul were besieged by poison ivy.

One evening we drove south out of Kearney to the sand pits that lie along Interstate 80. In the 1960s, when that highway was built across Nebraska, construction companies pumped gravel from the earth. Later the holes filled with water.

I was a strong swimmer, but Parker had never learned that art, so we stayed close to shore, floating and splashing like children. We were alone that night. No one else had chosen that time or that sand pit, and the light of the sun sinking into the cottonwoods and the faint breeze carried a message I could not deny. I crawled up into Parker's arms while he crouched in the waist-deep water and we held each other, quietly, for a long time, water lapping our shoulders, robins filling the air with good-night songs.

The next day I left for the Big Six, where I stayed for weeks. Alone. Parker and I talked by phone, and occasionally he drove the one hundred miles north into the hills to be with me, or I drove south and west to Kearney to rest in his arms at night, but I had withdrawn, and it was the right thing to do.

In my mind rests an image as stark and calm as a Japanese painting. Just off center stands a great blue heron, one leg raised as if stepping; it is tucked momentarily under the weight of the bird's body. The other leg sinks into the graying water of dusk. Cattails, bulrushes, spikesedge, pondweed all blur into shades of twilight, like layers of paint ceremoniously applied to the canvas.

I stand on the eastern shore of Lake Ericson, looking west toward the marsh and this scene. The sun's warmth still lights the horizon, although that luscious orb has slipped beneath the hills.

The adult great blue heron, if one could get close enough to measure, is taller than most grade-school children. Birds can reach four feet in height. Wings spread to six feet. Individual feathers can span close to ten inches from tip to tip, but these statistics hardly carry the magic of this bird when it presses wings against air, lifts its great bulk into flight, and floats on wind like a kite, long legs extended like a tail.

I have watched these birds for long minutes, not unlike a spy hiding in cover near shore, invading the private world of the great blue heron as it plunges its daggerlike bill into water, extracts a frog or fish. Swallows. Pauses. Steps. Seconds move like hours. The heron holds its pose, revealing no motion, until the next arc, the next flowing movement of bill toward water, swift, like the arm of a dancer unfolding, extending, retracting in the blink of an eye.

While the great blue heron nests in colonies, it spends most of its time a solitary creature, waiting and scanning the landscape for that which will fulfill.

RIPENING

It was still summer in the hills when I retreated to the Big Six, but I could feel fall in the air. Evenings were cooler; the dew on the lilacs and foxtail hung heavy in the morning. Dawn was crisp, the sky a clean, snappy blue. Sometimes in summer, mornings in the hills can be lazy and warm even at eight o'clock, a humming kind of haze clinging to the ground that foreshadows a day of intense heat, but now the air possessed a clipped quality, like a verb articulated with fine diction.

I revived my habit of walking early around the lake with a camera, making images of cabin doors and outbuildings, boats upturned on sawhorses, metal chairs nailed to docks, and bevies of dried leaves tucked into corners. I captured scenes that nudged me with a particular feeling about the land and this place. I did not think of this activity as part of my project. This was not research. Research was something done in libraries, in city records, in interviews. This wandering, inquisitive, open-eyed recording was simply me being in a place that evoked feelings of home. I saw these two activities as separate compartments of my life, like the two journals I kept, one for research and one for my heart. Only much later would I see the story was woven from both.

* * *

I started wearing a 1940s dress around the cabin. Years earlier, I had rummaged the dress from an attic in Oregon. It was all cotton, airy and loose fitting, a welcome change from the cutoffs and tank tops I usually wore. The material was of that petunia pattern associated with forties-style draperies, big cabbagelike flowers massing together in shades of pink and red, punctuated by the green of an occasional leaf. It was undoubtedly ugly, yet eternally funky in my mind, and one day I wore it out for a walk in the grassy open lots between the Big Six and my uncle's cabin and along the slough toward the Point. I felt like Heidi blithely skipping through fields of flowers, completely relieved of worldly concerns. I headed for my uncle's to pick some apples from his tree, which was laden with fruit. Instead, I surprised a man who appeared to be hiding in the tree. At first all I could see were his legs. He stood close to the trunk, as if he hoped he would blend with that part of the tree's anatomy. As I drew closer, he hurried away, edging Jim and Elaine's cabin until he reached the road, jumped into the driver's seat of a white car, and sped away. He had no box or bucket, so I did not think he had come to steal apples. I was frightened and no longer felt like a carefree part of the landscape. Instead, sensitized for danger, I became aware of every movement around me. I picked a few apples, cradling each in a portion of the dress that extended like an apron, but the spell was broken and I walked back to the Big Six, carrying my booty without joy.

The next morning I set out while sun still touched the eastern horizon. I drove toward Ericson on the River Road, straight through town past Spilinek Hardware, Pat's Market, the bank and gas station, and north toward the highway, where I turned west, picked up speed, then slowed for the bridge that crosses the Cedar. I let up on the gas and leaned my arm and head out the window to breathe deeply of the swampy smell that rises from the river. Just as you cross that bridge the smell will hit you, a rising draft of sweet, rotting, water-rich air, soaked with cedar, damp grass, and warmth.

Whenever I enter Ericson from the west, long away from this place, I stretch my head out the window and fill my lungs as I cross this bridge. Nowhere else on earth have I breathed this ripe, pungent, homebound air.

A half-mile west, I turned north on the road that leads to the Pitzer Ranch. The road follows the course of the Cedar as it meanders through the hills. Sunflowers crowded the edge of the narrow gravel road. Their arms reached four and five feet into the sky. All orbs of yellow turned to greet the rising sun. I inched along the thirty-mile road, absorbing the yellow blooms, the complete bliss of morning, the comforting freedom I felt alone in prairie, until the road simply stopped at Highway 11, north of Burwell in Garfield County.

Later that week, on an Indian summer day, I slipped into a bathing suit, pulled on one of my father's old cotton dress shirts, and sat on the back stoop to dump sand from an ancient pair of sneakers. I had a flashing memory of my mother sitting in the same position, same outfit, same intentions; only years separated us.

I walked east along the Big Six, through the break in the fence at the corner of the yard, and pushed across prairie grass fields toward the Point. Years ago my mother cut west across the yard, walked the tiny footbridge, and followed the slough toward the swinging bridge. But there was no swinging bridge anymore, another fact that separated this day from years of family ritual.

At the Point, I waded across a narrow, abandoned channel of the river. A new channel had pushed through on the far side of the island, and this old one was no longer deep or dangerous. The water reached my armpits, and I kicked into it. Two strokes and my feet again touched the soft bottom of the lake. In just steps I was up and out of water and into the marsh surrounding the island, which years before had been one bright heap of white sand. Now it was overgrown with cattails and bulrushes, and I was unable to walk its surface as I once had. Instead, I stepped into the gentle flow of the main branch of the Cedar. One last time this season I had to walk this river, and the memories of family walked with me.

Brown water pushed against my legs. I steadied myself with a long branch I had scrounged from the bank before crossing. On a sandbar I found two great blue heron feathers, which I worked into braids in my hair. How many years had my family walked this river? How many feathers had my mother gathered? How many walking sticks had my brother and father fashioned from cottonwood limbs?

Red-winged blackbirds flitted from bush to bush, crying my presence. Marsh wrens warbled. Far ahead on the bank stood a bird I could not identify. I waited. Soon it would rise and float away on wind, but it did not. I closed the gap between us. With its wings folded, bill dipped, it was clear the bird was not budging. At twelve feet I saw the eye—one golden eye, watching me. I let the river flow around my legs. The eye was fixed on my face. I moved laterally toward the bank, and that eye followed. For several minutes we stared at each other, and in that eye I saw a world of knowing, a world beyond perception, a world wild and unpredictable. Finally, I backed reverently down the shore of the sandy river, unwilling to test the bird's will. Heading home I was reminded of countless afternoons when my mother returned to the Big Six from a day on the Cedar, wide-eyed, out of breath, and full of story.

My father hired me to paint Sandcrest, Honey's cabin. He drove to Ericson with a car full of gallon paint cans—white for the trim and green for the clapboard—and I began the daily ritual of rising early for toast and coffee, then driving halfway around the lake to Sandcrest, where I parked in the shade and hauled a ladder slowly around the structure, climbing up and down and scraping peeling flakes of paint. I worked for only a few hours some days, driving back to the Big Six to shower, then sit at my desk and stare at blank paper. If I wrote anything it turned out to be a journal entry about the color of morning, the layers of birdsong showering from cottonwoods, and the smell of prairie blowing in off the lake.

Other days I spent all morning at Sandcrest, returning again after lunch and staying late into the afternoon and early evening when the shadows were long, the light low and yellow. During the day I tuned my portable radio to the only station I could pick up, a station from Ord where, of course, they played polka music. At noon there was a farm market report, and shortly before noon came a community call-in show where people advertised possessions they were selling—a saddle, sofa, tires for a truck—or inquired about objects they were seeking: baby clothes, a table saw, a mower. I went through periods of listening avidly to this thread of connection with the outer world and other times of refusing to consume even one more polka tune, opting instead for the sound of the earth: wind and leaves, voices far off across water, a lone dog, the noon whistle, birdsong, my own breath.

One fall day when the air was clean and the lake the color of sapphires, a flock of pelicans steamed south across that body of water, like a great white riverboat. I had never seen pelicans on the lake; I stopped work and ran to the bank, gasping: "Look! Look!" to anyone who would hear. But there was no one, and I watched from the bank like the only person on earth, witnessing essential beauty, unable to share it, a tangle of emotion grabbing at my throat. I worked on the west side of the cabin that morning, stopping often to check the birds' movements. They floated, one large, luminescent mass, south toward the dam, then chugged up-channel again toward the marsh at the north end of the lake. At noon, I drove back to the Big Six, made a sandwich, and perched on a wicker stool at the counter. From the kitchen I could just catch a glimpse of the lake through the bedroom window, and a wave of desire rolled over me—for the feel of outdoor work, for wind and air around my arms and legs like a pillow of comfort, for long hours spent near water with smells as fresh as birth, for a cascade of single moments sheltered beneath the wing of my grandmother's cabin, near to memories, near to hope.

Days later, while I was painting again in the shadow of Sandcrest, the delicately beautiful girlfriend of that roving cowboy walked by along the road. I called out, set aside the brush, and walked over to visit. It was midmorning and she had been gathering grasses and late-season flowers along the road. I had never seen her outside the setting of the Hungry Horse and the Saturday-night arena of carefully orchestrated attire. She wore a loose-fitting shirt and old shorts. Not a speck of makeup marred her face. She talked politely, a little unsure of herself, but sweet, and a solid sense of identification hit me: She was just like the small-town girls I had grown up with. Pretty, well-mannered, kind, a girl who had stayed close to home, a girl who had learned well the lessons of the country-and-western songs: Stand by your man. I saw in her a much younger, a much more hopeful me, and I was filled with empathy. I did not know the details of her relationship with the cowboy, but I had seen his behavior. He still drove by my house regularly, and I knew he would go as far as I would let him.

We chatted about the pelicans, about flowers and my work on Sandcrest; then she wandered on toward the house where she lived with her cowboy. I never saw her again in such a dressed-down state, but I felt closer to her from that day forward.

One afternoon I was standing near the top of the ladder at the peak of the roof on the back section of Sandcrest, an addition attached to the original structure shortly before Pop's death. The kitchen had been expanded and a small room with a shower and sink had been added to the bedroom.

I was brushing back and forth, balancing a coffee can full of paint on the top rung. The day was hot and perspiration gathered in the pockets below my eyes. Wisps of hair stuck to my forehead. I reached with the back of my hand to push them away. Instantly every inch of my body ached as if I had been smashed in a vise grip. I do not remember getting down from the ladder, but suddenly I was lying in the grass, clutching myself and rocking, dazed. When I got my senses, I realized I had brushed the electrical wire entering the house at the roof peak. I had let loose the coffee can, and paint was splashed across the yard. Only the ladder remained in position. I sat rubbing my arm. At that very moment a small company truck with the words "Loup Valley Public Power" on it drove toward me on the road, and I hailed the man in the cab, rising and lurching to his window to explain. He parked and got out, wearing thick rubber gloves and a hard hat, and climbed the ladder. He wrapped and bent the wires masterfully, climbed down, warned me to be careful, and drove his truck out of sight around the bend, like the Lone Ranger or a knight riding his white steed over the horizon. I sat on the front step for a few minutes collecting myself and rubbing my arm, then got a hose and washed down the spilled paint. Who was this man who had appeared as if on cue? I waited for his truck to return, but it did not, and I began to think his appearance was one of those curious twists of fate that bring people into our lives at exact, necessary moments, then eject them, like second-act characters whose roles are spent. How many other people, entering my life at pivotal moments, had been sent for reasons beyond my ken?

Only the back of the cabin remained to be painted, so I pushed on despite the ache in my arm. I was running low on green paint and had to soak up remnants from the bottom of each discarded can. When I reached the northeast corner and scraped the brush across the last board, I sighed with relief, dropped the green brush, grabbed a fresh one, dipped it in white paint, and swabbed above the door: "Lisa Dale 9/20/84." It was my claim on this place, this string of moments that would soon become the past. It was my testimonial, my act of bearing witness to all that had happened here, all I had felt, all I had heard on the wind and all that had entered my body as wisdom, as yet unrecognized but known in some deep part of me, beyond words, beyond reason, beyond logic.

I set out for Kearney to spend time with Parker. It was football season and a weekend, and I remember we listened to the Nebraska game on the radio, out in the yard, sipping Budweiser. Parker was building some stereo speakers for my car and he moved back and forth from the car to his work area. I followed. A sense of timelessness came over me, a remembrance of my childhood on autumn weekend days when my father would pace from house to workshop, cursing the Nebraska Huskers and jumping with delight when they did something good, muttering under his breath about the coach and the players and the wood he could not get to do what he wanted it to do, or a tool he could not find. Every radio in the house and another portable in the workshop was tuned to Lyle Bremser, KFAB radio's Husker football announcer.

"Man, woman, and child!" Bremser yelled, and I knew something tremendous had happened. A roar emanated from the radio. My father strained to hear Bremser's words explaining the play.

I slipped in and out of the moment with Parker and the memories of home, connecting the color of the light and the smell of burning leaves to my childhood and another Nebraska town, another decade, another football game. We sipped our beers and talked low, listening to the radio. Parker tinkered with his project. It was a sweet way to end a season, and I knew it was ending. So did Parker.

We piled into cars the next day with some friends and caravaned to a place along the Platte River where a woman lived alone with her brood of children. She had no electricity, cooked on a big iron cookstove with wood and used lanterns to light the house at night. I was fascinated. She was not a hillbilly. She was bright, and different, and her children were smart and individual, and she had chosen to live in these woods in a house without lights and without heat and without a man. Her couches were covered with quilts and there were hundreds of books on shelves and magazines in baskets. A row of windows opened onto the browning woods that surrounded her house. We spent the afternoon visiting. I walked in the trees along the river. What kind of life was this?

Later Parker said, "I took you there because I thought you'd like it."

"You were right," I said. "You were right."

The next image I can conjure is of Parker and me storming down some Sandhills highway. Up ahead sits a police car.

"Game check," Parker said.

"Huh?"

"They're checking for pheasants." His voice sounded tense.

"Well, we don't have any."

"Here, take the wheel." He started to scoot across the seat.

"Take the wheel? We're driving!"

"Take the wheel."

"Why?" We were speeding toward the police barricade.

"My license is expired."

"Oh, jeez, Parker."

We fumbled over each other as I worked my leg down to the gas pedal and settled into the driver's seat. We slowed for the barricade.

The officer strode to my window. "You haven't been hunting today, have you?" he asked, leaning down and peering in at us.

"No, sir," I said.

"May I see your license?"

"Yes sir." I rummaged in my purse and pulled my license from my wallet.

He put it close to his face and inspected it, looking at me.

I smiled.

"Well, you two have a nice afternoon," he said, handing me my license and bending down to look at Parker. "Pretty day," he said, straightening up

"Indeed it is, sir." I rolled forward, cranking the window closed.

"Expired," I said.

"Yep."

"What are you going to do about that?"

"Renew it."

"When?"

"Soon."

"Parker. Parker." I didn't say any more. In my heart I was already edging away.

October. I had watched three seasons roll past my life in the hills—the tentative late spring days of June, alive with lilac and wild iris, spilling into long summer days full of last light, and the contracting, clear, crisp mornings of autumn materializing as if from a puff of smoke, seeping in on these hills and the familiar, soothing warmth of summer.

I bundled in a robe on chilly mornings and carried a cup of coffee to my desk to watch the sun rise over the cottonwood trees east of the Big Six. I blew steam at the screens on the windows, still thrown open to outside air and birdsong. Daily I wrote in my journal. The book reserved for "Research" lay untouched. When the air warmed, I wandered the lake, read, wrote letters.

One day I remember dragging to the desk to write a first sentence; I was so full of distaste for myself that I simply could not stand it anymore. I cannot recall now what those first few words were, so many times rewritten since then, but I had begun, finally, the story I had said I would write, even though I did not know what I was trying to say, or how to say it, and the relief was immense. Once over the edge and into the work, I could not stop. I scribbled for days and pages, verbose and wandering prose. I told everything I knew and padded it as much as possible, assuming that longer was better.

Late one morning, simply bursting with words, a jumble of ideas, I ran from the cabin. Walk. Move. Perambulate. I did not know where I would go; I simply had to move through landscape. I sat on the back stoop, quickly tied a pair of hiking boots, pulled a bulky cotton sweater over my head as I hurried across the yard, and jumped in my car. I drove west toward town on the River Road, destination unknown. Just past the Foster ranch I swung south on the road to the dump and rumbled across the low plank bridge that fords the Cedar. A half-mile beyond, I parked along the side of the road, hustled through a deep ditch and up the other side, and crawled between the strands of a barbed-wire fence.

This area on the west side of Lake Ericson had been designated a wildlife refuge years ago by some county or state agency. I did not know the details; I just wanted to walk in untamed land. The bank overlooking the river was only yards ahead, and I set a course across the cactus- and bunchgrass-covered field to reach it, but the terrain was rougher than I had suspected. What from the road had looked like a flat field was really a hummocky pasture choked with waist-high grass and impenetrable sumac bushes. I had to backtrack several times to get through the brush to the river's edge.

Once there I gazed down on a brown-and-blue trail of sand and water, like an exquisite "S" brushed across the earth. The bank was steep. High water had cut deep into the dune. Bank swallows swirled in the sky above the river, diving and skidding toward holes in the bank. All was quiet, save for the voices of birds.

South I could see a wooded area. As children we had rowed across the lake to get to this thicket. Boys my brother's age had built forts and tree houses, from which they hurled threats if trespassers dared enter their sacred space. I had only been there once or twice as a child. Now, I forged across prairie to reach those trees.

The actual distance could not have been more than half a mile, but I must have walked well over a mile to get there. Up and down the earth tossed me. I had to tunnel inland, away from the river, to get around huge thickets of plum and sumac. My sweater was covered with brown burrs, but I felt compelled to push on.

I found openings in the landscape and worked back toward the riverbank, then south along its edge. Finally, I breached the last of the sumac-covered dunes. The land slid down, opening into a grassy slope and then a marshy area level with the lake. My overland course bisected a path that led from the woods toward water, ending at an abandoned duck blind and the last remnants of a stubby dock hugging the shore. A small lagoon separated from the main body of the lake lay before me. The water was flat, reflecting sky like a sheet of glass. I crouched in the cattails, quiet, waiting. I could feel something coming, out there in the air like a premonition ready to sail into this inlet, ready to change my life, but no ships appeared, no canoes or even rafts.

The angle of the light reminded me of afternoons in Osceola, before I attended school, when I was very young and spent my days at home with my mother. There was a particular time of day in the early afternoon when the sun angled in the south windows and the color of the light was intoxicating. I sat at the bottom of the stairs, knees to chest, waiting for it to transform the kitchen and dining room. That essence of light and emotion stayed with me as a body memory, and I sank into identical light on the banks of the inlet, wobbling in and out of then and now. Ultimately, the moment passed. I rose and walked up the path toward the woods, transfixed by some spell of memory. The sides of the trail were steep, blocking my view as I climbed the path. Just as I cleared the bank, I raised my head, anticipating a long view of trees, an image from childhood. Directly before me, ground level, sat a great horned owl. I froze. The bird's head rotated toward me. Its haunting eyes stared straight into mine; a fraction of a moment stretched into eternity, and then the bird spread its wings and with one magnificent push lifted itself into the branches overhead and was obscured from sight. I leaned against the bank and breathed.

Stepping lightly over downed branches and around piles of leaves, I moved through the terrain, scanning the branches above, but nowhere could I make out the shape of owl. I rested on a downed tree trunk. Peace settled around me. It did not matter if I saw owl again. The nervousness I felt at the Big Six was gone. I hiked toward the road. Just beyond the trees I encountered a man. He was carrying a rifle. We stumbled for words. I was alone in the land with a man with a gun, and my immediate response was to soothe him.

"Be nice; don't provoke him," my fight-or-flight response dictated, "and move away. Now."

I said everything I could think of to make him feel comfortable. I joked and chatted—who knows what I said?—all the while working my way toward the road. He walked with me, being equally friendly. As we neared the fence, we bade each other farewell, and I moved as quickly as possible, without running, toward the barbed wire, slid through the strands, leaped the ditch, and hit the road with relief. He was not behind me, but a car was approaching from the south. As it moved into view, I recognized it as that roving cowboy's pickup truck.

He coasted to a stop beside me. His girlfriend smiled from the passenger seat. I looked in the window and the cowboy leaned over toward me, "You need a ride?"

"Oh no, no, I'm just walking," I said.

"You sure?" His eyes were searching mine.

Did I look like a scared animal? "Yeah, I'm sure. I'm just hiking around enjoying the day. Thanks." I wanted them to leave, and yet I did not want them to leave. I did not want to be alone in the land with that man with his gun, but neither did I want to climb into the cramped cab with the cowboy who courted me and his live-in girlfriend.

I waved them on, thanking them, and set off at a good pace toward my car, which was down the road a couple miles. It didn't dawn on me for a long time, so intense was my fear of men and threatening situations, that the man in the woods was poaching. That land was a wildlife refuge. When I appeared, he was, no doubt, as scared of me as I was of him. I imagine now his interior monologue: "Oh my God, she'll turn me in. . . . I wonder if she knows who I am. . . . Who is she? . . . I better be real nice . . . walk with her . . . don't want to get arrested . . ."

Years later I am able to laugh when I remember this encounter. Now it rises as a comic scene, even though I wish I could go back and steer my car straight into town and notify the sheriff, but these are the latter-day reflections of a much more seasoned woman. Then, I was just damn scared.

For the next few weeks I wrote sporadically, but the story wandered. I did not know how to shape it. Story structure was still beyond my grasp.

The days grew darker and colder. At night I closed off the inner room of the Big Six and lit the furnace. By day I extinguished the heat and opened all doors—to porches and bedrooms where I kept the windows wide, unable to relinquish the essential parts of summer: sounds of the outer world, prairie air. The wind that rolled through the Big Six, though, was chill now, touched by fingers of winter. Dried cottonwood leaves rattled to the ground and covered the yard. The marsh grass that filled the north end of the lake faded golden brown and leaned low. I dug past my cutoffs to the bottom of the drawer and dressed in Levi's and sweaters. Late in the evening I tuned the black-and-white TV to the only station available, watched the ten P.M. news, then reruns of *WKRP*. I had not seen this sitcom when it was fresh, having given up television years before, but now I made it part of a nightly ritual, a shift that signaled to me I was becalmed, like a sailboat without wind. Still, though, I could not let go.

On a rainy day late in October a knock sounded at the back door of the Big Six. I peered out the window above the kitchen sink and did not recognize the pickup that sat in the drive. The knock came again. I lifted the curtain on the back door. A man I did not know stood outside in the wind.

I opened the door, leaving the screen between us.

"Yes?"

"Hi," he said. "My name's . . ." Something or other—a name I have now conveniently forgotten. His next line I will remember forever, though:

"I was wondering if you'd like to have a drink in town with me."

I must have stared at him blankly for seconds, a million emotions tumbling inside. "No," I said stiffly. "No, I don't care to. Thank you."

I was closing the door when he began his appeal: "Ah, come on, just one drink."

"No!" I closed the door.

I returned to the kitchen, incensed that someone I did not even know would have the audacity to walk onto my property and ask me such an invasive question.

I watched him retreat across the yard, climb into his truck, and leave. I went to the back door and locked it. I locked the screen on the front porch, too.

It wasn't long before the second knock came. I looked out the window expecting the same truck, but in the drive sat a different pickup, and this is where the memory goes foggy.

I have played this moment back so many times, revamping the script, writing in what I wish I had done, that I can no longer distinctly separate what actually happened from what I dreamed. As I recall, though—fighting for facts—I walked again to the door.

Outside on my stoop stood a different man, but with the same question.

Would I grace him with my presence at the Hungry Horse?

I declined, ever the good girl: "No, no, thank you so much, I'm busy, good-bye."

The story that rises more clearly in my mind, though, is a very different scenario, one I have imagined so many times that it begins to merge with truth. It is a script I would gladly play out if I could have that moment back again; it is the story I have written to redeem self-respect:

I reach above the refrigerator, lift the .22 rifle from the rack where it is stored, and prop the butt gently, naturally, on my hip. Then I walk slowly to the door, open it wide, and look that cowboy straight in the eye.

"Howdy!" I say.

The look in his eyes is one of terror.

"Get the hell out of my yard," I say, smiling broadly.

He raises a hand in protest.

I never move the gun from my hip, but something in my body says I can swing it into position with ease. I smile again and bare my teeth. "Move, sucker. Get the hell out of here."

And he does, with rapidity; he runs like a kicked dog across the yard of the Big Six, guns the motor of his Ford, and backs like crazy out the drive.

I wish I had done this, but I don't think I did . . . no, I don't think I did. Instead, I was nice, too nice for what the situation deserved.

The next day I lifted the rifle from the rack, slipped a box of shells into my pocket, and drove to the dump to shoot rats—an old form of entertainment I remember my mother and brother engaging in years ago. I am a good shot and I spent a lot of bullets, aiming at anything that struck my fancy: a jar, a bottle, a scurrying rat, a tin can.

Stan from the Hungry Horse drove up in a truck and backed into the dumping area. He climbed onto the flatbed and heaved bags of trash into the sandy hollows and piles of discarded goods: lumber and leaves, seeping garbage bags, boxes of clothes, dishes, broken baby chairs. He appeared to think it perfectly natural to find me at the dump with a gun, and I suppose in a land where hunting is revered, where there are annual seasons on deer, turkey, duck, and pheasant, where the taking of fish is a year-round occupation, where hunters make up a good part of the fall and winter trade, where the illegal chasing and gunning down of coyotes is weekend cowboy sport, the sight of me standing on the running board of my car, rifle in hand, spent cartridges at my feet, was not so odd.

I refrained from firing while Stan was there; he finished his work and we talked about business, the summer behind us and what the winter would bring. Already Stan was thinking ahead to the Fourth of July and the eleventh annual Turtle Races. He waved good-bye and drove north toward town.

I shot a few more rounds into the piles of refuse, but my anger was spent. I felt seduced back into a community of friends by easy conversation and our shared evocation of memory. I felt once again a part of Ericson, and no longer like some outsider, some woman alone—a woman men thought they could mark, like wolves mapping territory.

I wish I could write here that then I got up, packed my bags, went back to the university, submitted my masterwork, executed my exams, and was awarded highest honors for bravery in the field and for compositional excellence, but the fact is nothing so golden happened, and as for the details of what exactly did happen, they are part of the great unknown.

Somehow I broke out of the cycle of inaction, of TV sitcoms and unfocused days. How, though, I do not remember, except that Parker was pushing at me. I think he knew I would have to leave, that I would have to go back to Iowa and my studies, and so he pressed me for details: Would I come back? What would my studies bring me? Why was I pursuing a master's? Did I love him? All of these questions now seem calculated, positioned, to make me decide, lined up like ammunition to bring about some movement. And they worked. At the beginning of November I drove to Kearney to celebrate Parker's birthday, but in that visit, the end was imminent. We both could feel it, even though Parker was more jovial than ever, funny and sweet; he came home in the middle of the day, cap set sideways on his head just to make me laugh. He hugged me, and we planned a dinner out that night. Despite all this, I could see the sadness in the corners of his eyes. He was too happy, trying too hard.

I think that may have been what made me decide. I was hurting both of us too much. It was like putting an animal out of its misery when the end is near; I acted. I chose. I decided I had to go, and soon.

At Ericson, I talked with Stan and Clarence at the Hungry Horse. I had taken a lot of slides over the last six months, and suggested it would be fun to show them.

Stan said, "We'll make popcorn and advertise, and you come on in and show them like a movie."

We agreed on a date, and I began placing slides into a story line to map my adventures of that spring, summer, and fall in Ericson.

Whenever I saw people who rarely crossed my path, I said good-bye; I put in a change of address at the post office and the bank. I started to pack.

Finally the evening arrived, and I did my song and dance. The people loved the images, and there were plenty of laughs. When the night was over, I packed my projector and carousels of slides and drove for one of the last times down the moonlit River Road to the Big Six Country Club.

The next day I backed the car to the stoop. Teddi Spilinek stopped in the middle of the road when passing, left her car running, and walked to the fence. I met her there and she told me how much it had meant to have me in Ericson that summer. Her words were genuine, and I felt I had found a sister under the skin. We said good-bye slowly, neither wanting to be the first to turn, but I was operating within a dream at that time. I remember carrying it with me as I lugged books and bags to the stoop and heaved them into the back of the car: I believed I would be back, that it would all be the same again, that I was going away for only a little while, and so it was I who raised my hand first for the final wave. It was I who turned first and marched back to my car. I must have worn this dream the way a driver wears a safety belt. Any rational person would have questioned how I thought I would make a living in the hills. Did I intend to live in the family cabin? Did I intend to work as a barmaid for the rest of my life? I wasn't thinking in terms of such practicalities. I was thinking in terms of spirit, a return in spirit: My heart would guide me back, and the story I had lived with these people for the last six months would carry on, like a sequel to a movie. This thought comforted me, made the packing easier, made the inevitable leaving less sad.

I carried paper bags and hanging clothes to the stoop and loaded, packing carefully, fitting everything into its perfect slot in the rear of the car. Then I began closing the cabin: locking outbuildings, lowering windows, closing bangboards. My father would drive up later and drain the pipes and make final preparations for the winter freeze. It was the end of a season at the Big Six Country Club, the first time anyone in our family had stayed so late into the fall, warming the rooms and running the water.

I slept my last night in the bunk of my childhood, breathing the night air of Lake Ericson. I woke early, stripped the bed, loaded the last few items, and drove west, away from the Big Six and out of a chapter in my life it would take years to fathom.

In two hours I was in Kearney. Parker and I spent three days avoiding the inevitable. He grew quiet, and I grew overly talkative. Finally we parked ourselves on the picnic table in the back yard and cried, hugging and rocking. There were no words. I was leaving, and he knew better than I that I would not be back, that I was destined for other horizons.

"You work hard at that school," he said, his voice cracking. "Make something of yourself."

Such declarations seemed so distant from my feelings that I simply burrowed into his chest and arms and cried harder, not wanting to let go, but Parker made me sit straight in front of him, made me look him in the eyes. "I love you," he said. "Now go."

And I did. I got in my car and blindly, like a robot, drove south out of Kearney to Interstate 80, turned onto the eastbound ramp, and headed into the sun, Iowa bound, bound for a future I could not comprehend, bound for months and years of questions and confusion, bound for a serendipitous phone call, a teaching position on the banks of the Mississippi River, a generous grant to write about the Sandhills, and a book, far out there on the horizon, beckoning me like the long arm of summer.

The American plum, *Prunus americana*, grows wild from New England to Montana and south to New Mexico, Texas, and Florida. In Nebraska it grows in thickets along streams, lakes, or ditches, and in open prairie it hugs the sides of a sheltered hollow. In the hills, when branches burst with jewel-like fruit, people hike into fields and gather buckets full of the gems, which they carry back to kitchens and boil with water, stir with sugar, and decant into crystal jars—jelly the color of rubies.

All along the banks of Lake Ericson on Indian summer days, plums weighted the branches of thickets, tangled in sunburned leaves. In spring I watched an explosion and then a sweet fading of delicate white blooms; in summer I looked past the bushes, eye on the horizon; but in fall the fruit called to me, rich, ripe, and heavy: "Move quickly to harvest these treasures; they are forever fleeting."

PART THREE

WOMAN

ALONE

The history of my wandering is a circuitous yarn. I'd like to say I drove to Iowa and then six years later simply turned around and drove back into the Sandhills of Nebraska, but nothing goes in straight lines in my life. Instead, in 1986, after earning my graduate degree, I left the Midwest for Oregon—perhaps the twelfth time I had made that journey—and only came to be back in the heart of the country, and in the Sandhills writing this book, because of a curious twist of fate.

One day in late 1987 I returned to my southeast Portland apartment and found a message on my answering machine from the chair of the English department at Augustana College in Rock Island, Illinois. She wanted to know if I'd like a job.

Now, I had been considering returning to Iowa City, a short sixty miles via Interstate from Rock Island, but I had not made up my mind or sent out résumés, and I had never heard of Augustana College. I had come to believe, though, that opportunities are delivered when we need them, and I needed a chance at something new. I was working then as a journalist, writing other people's stories, and that work resonated like a tinny, sad tune in my life. This call from the blue had the scent of a miraculous moment, capable of transforming my life if I were willing to grasp the outstretched hand. I hesitated only momentarily, then reached and grabbed tight.

Two years later I found myself responsible for the entire journalism program of a small liberal arts college, teaching writing in the English department and struggling to meet the demands of an academic community. My reward? In 1989 I applied for a grant from the faculty research committee to travel western Nebraska, researching towns and history of the hills for a book—that old spinning out and reeling back again—and much to my surprise and delight, the committee awarded me a large chunk of money. The following summer I set out for the hills.

The sun is resting on top of the cottonwoods as I enter Broken Bow in Custer County. It has been a blistering day of heat pushing in at the windows and forcing through the fire wall between the engine of my car and the driver's seat. I have driven well over five hundred miles through endless, hypnotic prairie, drawn on by big sky and evocative curls of cirrus clouds. I have followed no itinerary. I have simply looked at the map and gone where I have not been. Today I traveled a dozen roads—state highways and sand ruts—and as I cruise west into this Sandhills town I feel wizened, dried from the heat and wind and sun and miles upon miles without water. I watch as a woman up ahead leans from her sidewalk into the street, sweeping the curb. She is silhouetted by sun, her figure a thin dark form against a huge sunburnt sky. Dust swirls into air.

Broken Bow is a town I remember from years ago. We were traveling as a family, going somewhere in the hills. The day was rainy and gray. We stopped in a town with a name that said "Way Out West" to me, a town bordering on Indian territory: Broken Bow. We parked along the curb outside a downtown café. I can see the lay of the land perfectly in my mind: brick streets, brick buildings, hovering gray sky. As a unit we scooted through rain and into the warm interior of the café. The place had beige Formica tables, high Naugahyde booths, and red menus sheathed with plastic. We sat at a round corner table, and I ordered a hot beef sandwich.

I look for that café as I drive through town now. It was on the south side of the street, facing north on the east end of a block of storefronts—I'm sure of it. I drive slowly and study each building, but the restaurant is nowhere to be found.

At the Wagon Wheel I drive the alley behind the motel to check for windows. During my travels I've identified the ideal out-back motel as one that evokes the Nebraska of my childhood. It will be a one-story frame building with a gravel parking lot. Windows will march across the front of the complex, and in the back, a row of windows, ensuring cross-ventilation in the rooms, will line the wall. The Wagon Wheel passes the test.

Inside I push open the front window, then prop up the small back window with a newspaper. Air slips through my room. The sound of robin's song cascades in, and for one brief moment I imagine I live in a cottage in these hills, that I am part of this land. I unload and soak the long miles out of me in a hot bath in a deep tub, letting the sound of running water, like the sound of wind in cottonwoods, carry me into remembrance.

Earlier in the month, in Ogallala, I hunted for an old lounge. It was a long narrow building with wide windows that faced a well-traveled street. I looked everywhere but couldn't find it. Years before, I had been traveling with my father. I was a little girl—how old I cannot say, and why we were out and about in Nebraska, just the two of us, father and daughter, only history knows. We stopped in a western town, a town steeped in the mystery of times gone by, of times my father revered, of times he taught me to hanker after with yearning and curiosity. We went to a lounge. My father had a drink. I probably had a Shirley Temple. On the wall there were the biggest horns I'd ever seen, long and twirled from tip to tip. My father told me about the cattle drives, how they'd pushed north from Texas and stopped right in this town. "One hundred years ago, cowboys wearing chaps and dusty kerchiefs swigged whiskey in this very bar." His arms swept the air of the dimly lit room.

I searched for that lounge for days, as if it were a critical link in my entry to these hills, as if finding it would show me the way into this story, guide me as I tried to know what it was I sought, but it was nowhere in any of the towns I traveled. Only much later in North Platte, when I came up over a viaduct, did I find it. It stretched for an entire block on the east side of the street, a long, low building with wide windows, but it was vacant. A realtor's sign hung crooked in a cobwebbed window.

Robins singing good-night songs outside my window bring me back to the Wagon Wheel. I realize I am being seduced by memories, that the task at hand has slipped behind the mirage of the past. In Nebraska it is difficult for me to detach, to look at the land clinically, to objectively gather data. This place is lined with my stories. It has the power of home, and any tale I can tell is woven with knowledge I carry from a childhood spent exploring sandy prairie.

I rise early at the Wagon Wheel the next morning. The sky in the east is pink with a yellow rim. Robins sing good morning. I pack and drive to Broken Bow's City Café for breakfast. All booths are full. The sign says, "Help Yourself to Coffee," and so I do, then slip into a seat at the counter, but not before I catch the eyes of several women occupying seats along the walls of booths. They stare, creases pulling their frowns low. They inspect me, then look away when I meet their gaze. I wonder if I have forgotten to dress thoroughly, but I catch a reflection of myself in the milk cooler, and it is just me.

After breakfast, I drive north and west into the hills on state Highway 2, a road I know will take me quickly into the kind of rolling prairie I crave. In Dunning, where the Dismal and Middle Loup rivers converge, the color of morning light, a thick covering of moss on roofs and a damp musty smell remind me of Ericson, and I cruise slowly over the two or three streets that make up downtown, sliding back and forth between memories and forward movement, trying to keep this new trip in focus, to understand how to do the kind of research I have said I will do.

By the time I reach Thedford it is late morning and the sun is high and hot. I pull off at the Arrowhead Café for an iced tea. The one-room café is small and cool, the air-conditioning a welcome relief from the blazing sun and parched prairie air. I take a seat at a small table near the door. The restaurant is full, and while most faces turn my way when I open the door, most people turn back to their plates and conversations after I enter. Most, except for the woman in yellow. She sits with her male companion at a two-person table below the west windows. They are facing each other. I am positioned so that I am facing them. She wears a daffodil-yellow dress, a black-and-white polka-dot scarf around her neck, dangling plastic earrings, and white pumps. He wears slacks and a short-sleeved oxford. It is the woman, though, who captivates my attention, as clearly I captivate hers; she can't quit staring, and so I watch her watch me. As I settle into my seat, her lips draw together. Her spine straightens. Her companion becomes remarkably interested in his plate. The woman elevates her chin, cuts a small piece from her plate, glances my way, then chews daintily. I don't know whether to laugh or cry.

I realize it is Sunday, and most of these folks have just been to church. To them I must appear inappropriate, dressed in a way that does not honor the Lord: I wear shorts, a tank top, and sandals. My hair runs in two thick braids down the sides of my head. Large sunglasses shade my eyes. And I am alone; I am an unescorted woman on a Sunday in Nebraska's outback, and that perhaps is a greater sin than the clothes I do or do not wear.

What the woman in yellow does not realize is that for me these circumstances are a victory. To be alone, braving the fear that has gripped my throat since the day I was dragged from a city street and strangled until I begged for air, to be alone choosing my destiny, is an act of will, an act of sheer determination. But how can I tell her? How can I explain that what she sees is not the whole picture, that the woman she judges is just me, coming up from the depths and defying the power of a person who considered ending my life, a man who in a few short minutes grabbed such power over my future that for years I watched behind me and measured my choices by the panic that crept up through my consciousness? Ever since I stopped drinking, stopped burying the truth of my fear and sadness, I have been forced to choose my steps knowing that at each turn some threat could cut me down. To choose to be out in prairie alone was a difficult act of courage. She could not see this, though. She could not know my story, and to tell the truth, I could not know hers, either. I could not know what made her straighten her spine and look furtively over her shoulder at me, pursing her lips and lifting her nose. I could not know the story that shaped her life, dictated her decisions; I could not know the events that had led her to wear a daffodil-yellow dress and black-and-white polka-dotted scarf on a Sunday in Thedford, Nebraska.

At the time, though, all this seasoned reflection escaped me. When I walked to my car, unlocked the door, rolled down the windows, then realized that the woman in yellow and her companion had stopped eating and were sitting tall in their chairs to watch through the glass, anger flared. I stepped away from the car, jutted my hip, slapped my hands to my waist, and spoke toward the window: "Take a good look." They averted their eyes. There was little joy in this defiance, in spinning through gravel in the parking lot, hurrying to get away from her, wanting only to put distance between us. I drove west toward Mullen, angry, hurt, and ready for something holy.

Five miles south of Mullen, on Highway 97, I took an unnamed side road—a thin line on state maps—that supposedly led toward the Dismal River. I had read about the Dismal, about how early ranchers had built their homesteads along its banks, far from any settlement. Even today the river is mostly inaccessible. Roads in the region cross it in only four places along its hundred-mile length. Two are state or federally maintained roads. The others are called "Narrow Paved" or "Other All Weather."

It was midday—flat, white light, no shadows. Through the open roof of my car, sun baked my skin. Outside, heat dried the bunchgrass painting the hills a uniform beige. I passed a lone deer standing in prairie without cover. Some people would not have called this trail a road; the map indicated that up ahead it ended at the north fork of the river and did not appear again for several miles farther on, at the south fork. Something existed in between, and I did not care if it was only sand, a cow pasture, some rancher's rangeland. To me that unmapped stretch of prairie was a path into wilderness, and I wanted to be there.

At the end of the road the Dismal meandered east through stark terrain. Willow bushes hugged the banks; swallows dove at brown water under a rickety bridge. A hill rose on the far side of the stream, and I parked the car in front of a metal cattle grate embedded in the sand at the end of the pavement. Being there was like holding my breath waiting for an explosion that was imminent, but never came. There was only the bite of horseflies, the whoosh of swallow wings, a kind of hum in the earth, like the buzzing in your ears when the pressure changes. I cleared my ears, but the buzz persisted. I took a picture, only because I knew I would need confirmation of this place later. Then I cranked the engine and set my course for the uncharted region.

Cattle, yucca, pricklepoppies, and bluestem stretched out on all sides of a single-lane sand rut. A cow nursed her calf in the middle of the road. She lumbered away at the last moment, before I would have to stop, before I would sink in the soft sand. I don't know where I learned to drive in sand. Maybe it's just common sense, but I know you don't stop. Once I was out in that wallow, that was it. I couldn't even recall the last ranch road I'd passed. A walk out would be scorching. Instead, I just kept whipping the wheel this way and that, pushing my car through the deepest spots by flooring it. It was like a prayer in which I lost myself.

Nine miles later I emerged into a lush valley. A rancher worked fence from a pickup not far from the road. A semblance of pavement returned to the narrow path. A long-billed curlew swooped at my car, crying and diving as I spun out of sand and my wheels grabbed at the broken chunks of asphalt. Ten, maybe twenty miles farther on, a stop sign and a highway materialized. I felt like some Oregon Trail pioneer exuberant at the end of the day, when the destination loomed on the horizon. I stopped, got out—felt earth beneath my feet—then turned the car to the west and hit the gas, thinking water every mile. Within minutes a small stand of roadside trees caught my eye, and I swung into the gravel parking lot. A mourning dove gave her sweet, soft hoot. Wind caught the leaves of a Siberian elm. In the shade stood a rusty pump. At the base someone had scrawled in red paint: "40 pumps for water." I worked the arm ferociously . . . twenty-nine, thirty . . . thirty-nine—water gushed onto the sandy soil. In went one leg, then the other. I lifted handfuls to my face. The sharp iron flavor rolled from my mouth. I filled a bottle and drank long and hard, then splashed water into the air, christening this place and my life. It was one of those moments when you know you are in the right place, that your life is blessed. I sat on the picnic table and drank in the afternoon sky, the wind and air, the sheer joy of being in these hills, alone, by choice.

Miles west waited the little town of Arthur, seat of—and sole town in—Arthur County. I had been there before, searching for a church built from hay bales. That day was not unlike today: sultry; thunderheads building on the southwest horizon. Down a side street I bumped into some people from Canada. They were driving a huge motor home. In the road they stretched arms and legs, shaking out the stiffness of long miles. I parked behind them, and as a group we crossed the road and circled the white stuccoed church, grunting as we passed each other, cupping our hands to windows to peer inside. "Never heard of a hay bale church," one Canadian said. "But I'm sure glad I've seen one." They piled into their motor home and roared away. The sound of their vanishing engine died back into a soft rustle of cottonwood leaves. I waited there, as if expecting some guest, leaning against the hood of my car, watching wind chase leaves and push puffs of sand across the road, feeling some essential connection rising within me.

Now I leave behind the pump and roadside oasis, angling west toward Arthur, drawn on by memories of white-washed stillness at Pilgrim Holiness Church. Something in that place beckons, some essence of landscape. South of town I pull in at the Cactus Flat Golf Course, buy two 7-Ups, and drink them standing in place. No customers fill the restaurant, and the kitchen help is camped at a table in the corner smoking Marlboros and watching TV. I drive north up Main Street. At the church I pause and frame a picture, then lower my camera and enter a familiar world. The only sound is of cottonwood leaves rustling in the wind.

I met my first long-billed curlew in May, early in this summer journey, when I was on my way to a branding in Garden County. Alice and Ed Dentler and I were driving south on a road locals affectionately call the Boulevard, a cracked and blistered trail of asphalt leading south from Lakeside. We were riding in the Dentlers' pickup truck, pulling a horse trailer, heading to Rich and Linda Sutphen's ranch a few miles south of Lakeside. A curlew glided above a field paralleling our path, and Ed told me local lore holds that after the curlews arrive in the spring there will be three more snows.

Curlews are like no other bird I have ever seen. Adults can stand about two feet tall. They are pale brown with markings of black and dark brown, and they have slender, bare legs, like the other shorebirds to which they are related, sandpipers and snipes, but they have a bill that distinguishes. It is sickle shaped and long, curving downward in one soft compelling arc, like a descending melody. Bills can measure as long as eight inches in adults, and in baby curlews the bill is often bigger than the chick's body. In flight curlews trail their legs behind them like great blue herons. With wings spread wide they dive at passing vehicles, screaming, "Cur-lew! Cur-lew!," each raucous vocalization rising in inflection.

At the Sutphen ranch, neighbors, some on horseback, gathered in open prairie around a line of pickups until the signal was given and a group of riders set off across fog-shrouded prairie. We traveled to three corrals that day, where cows and calves were rounded up, the calves branded, cut, dehorned, and vaccinated. About noon we gathered in a building not far from the Sutphens' house, where food was piled on card tables and Rich's workbench. After consuming the feast, adults kicked back to visit, and kids started a water fight in the yard. "It's a good life," Rich said that day, and I guess the curlews know it too, because they return each spring to these sandy hills from as far south as Guatemala to nest and raise their young. Many think the curlews are so wise, they set their ranching clocks by them. "When they leave in August," Alice told me once, "it's time to get your hay in."

THE

SHADY

REST

After leaving Arthur I drive south and west and check in at the Shady Rest Motel in Oshkosh. My reasons for being here are simple: I have a desire to stay in an old Nebraska highway motel, and this spot fits the bill. Both the Mormon and Oregon Trails passed by here. Decades later pavement was laid along the path. Generations of travelers have passed this spot. Here I find a deep connection to those who have gone before. My trip through the hills is built on such whims. There is no grand plan to my research. I am guided by intuition.

The next day I climb high into prairie above Ash Hollow State Historical Park along this byway, now named Highway 26, which follows the Platte River through Nebraska, as the earlier trails did. One hundred and forty years ago at Ash Hollow emigrants rested in the shade of ash trees along the banks of the North Platte River. The bulk of their Plains journey was behind them. Ahead lay the Rocky Mountain portion. Here, though, they could rest for a few days, repair wagons, visit with other pioneers, draw fresh water from the spring, gather wood in the hollow. Perhaps game would be shot.

The first experience of winching wagons through rocky terrain was just behind these travelers. At Windlass Hill, above Ash Hollow, wagons had to be winched three hundred feet to the floor of the canyon. Today I hike to the crest of that hill and look out across surrounding prairie. Spinning out in all directions are remnants of the Oregon Trail. One hundred and forty years since wagons streamed west, ruts from wheels that rolled across the Great Plains are still visible on these hills. Two-lane barren tracks branch out across green prairie like spokes in a massive wheel. Why hasn't grass grown up to obscure this trail? Why are these tracks still etched across the surface of earth, visible for all to see?

To the north and west stretches high Plains prairie, the southern extension of the Sandhills. I see in the distance the beginning of those sandy hills. I see also plowed prairie and topsoil blowing north and east with the prevailing wind. Sand and soil are lifting in waves and filling the air. Dust clouds pulse across the horizon.

Perhaps these Oregon Trail ruts persist to remind us of the mistakes made as we moved west and took the land. These hills should never have been plowed. Sandhills prairie is marginal land in terms of row crop agriculture. The soil is not as fertile or productive as land in the eastern prairies of Iowa and Illinois. And rainfall in this area seldom reaches twenty inches a year, hardly making it a farmers' paradise. Without irrigation this land would support little more than plants native to mixed- and short-grass prairie—grama, buffalo grass, bluestem, grasses suitable for grazing. I have seen so much irrigation in these hills on this journey, so much corn where it does not belong, so much plowing of sandy soil, that I am puzzled. What would it mean for this land if water used to irrigate these acres simply were no longer available?

Yesterday, driving south from Arthur, I passed Lake C. W. McConaughy, or Big Mac as they call it, which is not a lake at all, but rather a huge reservoir formed from the damming of the North Platte River. Kingsley Dam holds back 1.7 million acre-feet of water, an impossible amount to imagine. Perhaps more easy to grasp are the beaches. Flooding land above Kingsley Dam created a body of water with one hundred miles of sandy beaches.

I eat a late lunch at the Lewellen Café and return early to the

Shady Rest in Oshkosh, where I will spend another night. It feels like a day for pondering, and I haul a straight-back chair onto the stoop outside my door into the shade of a sprawling cottonwood tree, where I soak up late afternoon sun and gaze across river-bottom farmland toward the southern banks of the North Platte River.

Kingsley Dam was built in 1941, one of those Army Corps of Engineers projects that so many thought would transform the West into an oasis. Since then water has been shunted all over the state through a complex set of canals that have delivered water far from the banks of the Platte. This water has allowed farmers to cultivate crops like corn in places that without that water could never sustain such crops. The economy of Nebraska is built on this kind of agriculture. Nebraskans have come to think of their state as one of the primary corn-producing states in the farm belt. The truth is, though, that without an elaborate system of irrigation, crop yields would fall; there would be no burgeoning farm economy. The natural rainfall of this place could not sustain the crop.

I have mixed reactions when I consider these facts. While I feel allegiance to the state where I was reared, to the small towns and good-hearted people who make their living from the land, I also question allocation policy for water on the Plains and watch with sadness the impact of those decisions.

The Platte River is a shadow of what it was when pioneers drove teams of oxen along its shores. It was wide and treeless and full of water. Now, with all the dams—well over a dozen between Rocky Mountain sources for North and South branches and the Missouri River, where the Platte ends—flows have been reduced by such a degree that the riverbed has filled with sandbars covered with cottonwoods, elms, willows, and ash trees, sandbars that just eighty years ago were yearly scoured clean by annual rushes of snowmelt that pushed down the Platte from Wyoming and Colorado. They have become so wooded that they are permanent islands in the heart of a once-vibrant river. Now the Platte is little more than a braided stream of narrow channels trickling across Nebraska. As more and more water has been drawn, habitat for birds traveling the central flyway has been dramatically reduced. Sandhill cranes, which once rested along three hundred miles of the Platte's length in Nebraska, have been restricted to an eighty-mile stretch of the river where they can still find the conditions they need for feeding and courtship, the annual Nebraska part of their migratory journey north to Arctic nesting grounds.

The cranes have been using the Platte for millennia. In only eighty years we have almost annihilated their habitat. Once whooping cranes rested on the Platte, too, but these great birds are now practically extinct. Their loss marks an imbalance in our eco-system, like the loss of the salmon in the rivers of the Pacific Northwest.

Warm golden sun washes the banks of the Platte. The sky turns peach, and trails of pink rake the horizon. Watching this land move into night evokes images of Oregon Trail traffic, that breathtaking migration of three hundred and fifty thousand people in twenty-six years. Many stopped in Nebraska, bailed out on the overland journey, opted to stake a claim in the fertile Platte River Valley. Those homesteaders are the forebears of my state, the visionary men and women who began the whole water-sharing game. Little did they know what lay ahead.

Those same homesteaders started the little towns I travel in my journeys, the little towns that evoke for me a sense of family and community, that ring with an essence of small-town life I harbor deep inside: lazy evenings in cotton shirts, resting on doorsteps in fading light, weed-lined sidewalks, abandoned storefronts, muddy pickups, country music, horses, the scent of freshly cut hay.

How can I resolve my growing sense of contradiction? The very things I love about Nebraska—small towns, ranching, an independent spirit—are at root responsible for the problems the state now faces. It is settlement itself that has degraded this land, and my family was part of that settlement.

How can I say I question farming practices and yet say I love small farming towns? How can I revere the lifestyle of the prairie hamlet and yet deny the people who live there the ability to make a living so that they can remain on the land? These are vexing questions I cannot resolve. Instead, my mind wanders. Tomorrow I will follow the Oregon Trail along the North Platte River into northwestern Nebraska, to Scottsbluff and Mitchell Pass, to Agate Fossil Beds and Fort Robinson, places resplendent with childhood memories.

There is one plant in the Sandhills listed as an endangered species under the Federal Endangered Species Act: Hayden's penstemon, perhaps Nebraska's rarest wildflower. Sometimes called blowout penstemon, this native perennial grows only in sandy blowouts, those areas in the hills blown bare by wind, all vegetation scoured away by sand. It is the only endemic plant in Nebraska, which means its range is restricted to a specific locale. And it is one of few endemics on the Great Plains.

A member of the figwort family, which includes the foxglove and snapdragon, Hayden's penstemon sprouts flowers in densely grouped clusters at the top of stems that grow to thirty inches tall. Each cluster holds four to six very fragrant flowers, some pink, others a milky blue. This plant thrives in the first stage of plant succession when blowouts begin to heal. When grasses begin to take over, though, it cannot compete. Once Hayden's penstemon thrived in the Sandhills, because there were so many blowouts, but since wildfires have been controlled and the herds of buffalo destroyed—two elements of the natural world on the Great Plains that regularly disturbed the soil and promoted blowouts—Hayden's penstemon has become increasingly rare. Ranchers in the region do such a good job of keeping the mantle of grasses intact that few opportunities for blowout penstemon to take hold exist anymore.

It seems ironic that the very practices that preserve this prairie are the practices that now drive Hayden's penstemon toward extinction, but that is like this place, where traditions embodying contradictory elements are part of a culture of ranching, of making a life on the land.

OLD

ROAD

I check out of the Shady Rest early, when the sun's rays are still parallel with land and dew rests on grasses and spiderwebs. I drive west on Highway 26, moving into soft yellow light, traveling the same valley trail pioneers followed west. For the first time on this journey I have a distinct course, one that will parallel an earlier journey made with family years before.

The sky is cloudless and hawks watch fields from high atop telephone poles. West of Oshkosh a huge cattle-feeding operation sprawls north of the highway. The stench of unhappy animals permeates the morning. I speed past, wanting to ignore the realities of agriculture in Nebraska. Right now it seems easier to just be in the land, to explore, chase memories. Memories are easy compared to the task of solving problems revolving around land-use issues, so I indulge myself and drift back into the stories of my childhood. Perhaps there are keys inside these memories, keys to a way I can affect the future of this land I call home.

In Broadwater I cross to the south side of the Platte and approach Courthouse Rock and Jail Rock, two well-known landmarks along the overland trail. Emigrants thought the bulky shapes of clay, rising from the horizon, looked like their namesakes in towns back east. A few miles farther west, in Morrill County, Chimney Rock looms, harbinger of hardships to come. Part volcanic ash and part Arikaree clay, this towering landmark has signaled to travelers for centuries that the Plains portion of their journey is almost over, that the rugged mountains lie ahead.

I remember this monument from 1966, the summer of our great adventure through Nebraska, when my father and mother and brother and I traveled western Nebraska discovering the history of our state. We pulled to the edge of the road. The day was windy. My father steadied me as I perched on the running board, gazing across prairie to that finger of earth jutting skyward, story spinning in my mind, wind in my ears, meadowlarks on wind.

Between Bridgeport and McGrew I pull off at a viewing area for Chimney Rock, but the raw experience I remember from my childhood is erased by a paved parking lot and a billboard proclaiming the coming attraction: an interpretive center with guided exhibits that will walk visitors through the pioneer experience with painted images and remnants of trail memorabilia housed behind glass. To me it feels as foreign as Disneyland. I cannot halt this march of progress, but there must be something I can do that will shape the way this land is inhabited in days to come.

I swing back onto the road. All along this section of Highway 26 the stories of westward expansion come to life. The route of the Pony Express passed near here, as did the Sidney-Deadwood stage route, the Mormon Trail, the Oregon Trail, and the Texas Cattle Trail pushing north to Montana. Here, too, along the banks of the Platte, emigrants scratched the words "post office" in soft sandstone and left letters for travelers who would follow in weeks and months to come. Pioneer cemeteries and solitary graves flank the ruts of the Oregon Trail. This history is intriguing, and I allow myself to be caught up in the story. Exploring the past lets me avoid the realities of today. I pull off in McGrew and make photographs of two contemporary artifacts soon to be part of the great sweep of history: the McGrew Merchant Company, with two aging gas pumps shaded by a lone Siberian elm, and the two-story McGrew Lounge across the street with its flat pink-brick facade. In an arch above the central door the words "Pink Palace" are painted, and in similar script arching above each ground-floor window are the names "Duane" and "Dora."

It is late morning by the time I see Scottsbluff Monument on the horizon, another destination I remember from the summer of 1966. We hiked to the top that summer as my father told the story of another summer day some thirty years before, when he and his brother, my uncle Jim, were visiting relatives in the town of Scottsbluff. It was the 1930s, long before trails had been carved to the top of the bluff. The two boys pawed their way up to the tunnel that joins the east and west faces. The way my father tells the story, they entered the tunnel from opposite ends. It was dark inside, and their eyes adjusted slowly to the shade. As they walked toward each other, they heard a noise that stopped them on tiptoe. My father looked down. There in the middle of the rock floor lay a rattlesnake, coiled and giving its warning. He says they didn't even hesitate; each turned and shot out the end of the tunnel and straight down the face of Scottsbluff, stumbling and flying to the plain below. It was a wonderful story for a little girl climbing that bluff, a story imbued with adventure and danger, the kind of story that shaped my young images of Nebraska as a rough-and-tumble world.

By the time I reach the base of Scottsbluff the sun is high. Construction equipment occupies the parking lot near the visitors center. Neatly paved trails provide access to the bluff. I set off at a good pace. The temperature is in the nineties, and heat reflects off the buff-colored rocks, turning the air to an oven. Near the top memories flood back. I check the ground and move into the cool darkness of the tunnel. A bright circle of light draws me toward the other end. Outside I shade my eyes and scan the land below. The towns of Scottsbluff and Gering sprawl onto the surrounding plains: housing developments, factories, and acres of irrigated fields. I work to conjure that old notion—that this land was once part of a great saga—but it looks so tame.

*   *   *

I strike a course north on Highway 29 into high Plains prairie, away from Scottsbluff and the old Oregon Trail and toward Agate Fossil Beds, where, years before, my family spent hours exploring, scratching in dirt. My father said the area had once been an inland sea, and the tiny shells lodged in spires of earth seemed to bear out his story.

North of Mitchell I turn off Highway 29 onto a gravel road paralleling the Niobrara River which leads toward the Beds. Once there, I discover a trailer has been dragged in to serve as a visitors center. Huge wheelchair-accessible rest rooms have been constructed near the gravel parking lots. Lumber and bags of cement lie everywhere. I search for a path into the Beds but discover they are now off-limits. A display in the temporary visitors center points to soil and rock formations I could inspect if I could get into the land. I leave quickly, driving into backcountry down a chalk-colored road, eating dust. Soon I am in piney hills I cannot find on the map, and in being lost, I feel right for the first time in miles. I cross a wooden bridge; a narrow but full river flows beneath. The next turn weaves north to Highway 20 and to Fort Robinson State Park, a place my family stayed in 1966, renting one of the white frame houses that had once been officers' quarters. At the fort I check into a room in the lodge, reminding myself that this is a new journey. Still the question nags: How can these memories serve to shape the future?

In my room I wash out clothes in the bathroom sink, draping shirts and shorts from towel bars and curtain rods. From my window I have a view of the buttes to the west, and I hole up to read. Later I explore the lodge, reacquainting myself with fort history. Fort Robinson was established in 1873 as an Indian agency where U.S. government goods were dispensed to Native Americans in the area. This was after the time that the Sioux had been restricted from their native grounds, but before they had all been herded onto reservations. At some point, troops were dispatched to protect the agency. The place was turned into a prisoner-of-war camp during World War II. Finally, it became a state park.

The next morning I cross the field in front of the lodge to visit the fort museum, where I gaze at displays of Indian shirts and war-bonnets, soldier guns and early fort cookpots, working my way through the story the museum has constructed about Fort Robinson and western Nebraska history, but the tale it tells—which paints the taking of this land as a God-given right—invokes my anger, and I write a short retort in the guest book blasting their biased interpretation: white-man history. Fort Robinson is the place the Sioux warrior Crazy Horse was killed. Some would say he was murdered in the guardhouse by representatives of the U.S. Army. I cannot speak the truth of this situation, but my heart tells me this is not the glorious place of childhood perceptions.

Just as I search for the boundary between sentiment and sentimentality, I must try to understand where the usefulness of a memory ends. What purpose do these stories serve, which rise from my childhood and haunt me as I travel these hills? Even though I see that progress has changed the places I once traveled, even though I see that now I interpret these places differently, I cannot give up the belief that these memories, burning like lamps in the night, shine through to me for a reason. Embedded in each there must be some lesson. Could it be as simple as the power of those things we love rising to remind us that we must name them? If I do not name those things I love, who will know what is worth saving and what can be let go? I love the rawness of Nebraska. I love the landscape speaking for itself, untouched by interpretive centers; I love the miles upon miles of open prairie, the grasses, the weeds, the wild-flowers. I love the sandy dunes, the abundant water, and the lakes and birds the water brings.

I name these things because I do not want to lose them.

𝒩OTEBOOK: HAWKS

Hawks have guided me through these hills. Time after time a sighting of a red-tailed, Swainson's, or ferruginous hawk has sent me toward my next discovery, into my next adventure. Once I followed a red-tailed hawk as it soared in tight circles above prairie. Something told me to keep watching, and so I turned my car onto a nothing road and crawled along, glancing up through the sun roof, keeping an eye on the hawk. Abruptly it dove, talons extended, then rose from the grass with a small animal in its claws. It flapped away across the road and out of sight.

Hawks belong to a large family birds that includes osprey, kites, harriers, and eagles—birds of prey. Most hawks seen in the Sandhills fall into a category called buteos, hawks that soar in search of prey. Sandhills hawks hunt rabbits and mice, snakes, grasshoppers, and sometimes even birds. They are calculating creatures with extraordinary eyesight. While humans have one fovea—the area on the retina of the eye where light rays reflected from objects converge—hawks have two. Consequently, distant objects that look fuzzy to our eyes can be seen with absolute clarity by the hawk.

It makes me wonder, then, what they saw in me one day. I was bumping down a sand path in the middle of prairie somewhere in the hills when I approached two hawks sitting on adjacent fence posts. They were perhaps ten feet from my car and the road I traveled, but they did not budge. Each in turn, as I passed, zeroed in on my eyes with its eyes and watched me as I moved from left to right, its head moving with my movement. It was an unnerving moment of focused awareness, of watchfulness. I drove on without moving an unnecessary muscle, holding the wheel steady, remembering the red-tailed hawk of my earlier journey and thinking of the open sunroof above my head.

Later, when a fork appeared in the road, I steered absently in the direction of the fence posts where the hawks had sat, so powerful was the memory of their presence. The road took me through sixty miles of range where I did not see another human; sixty miles filled with box turtles, lark buntings, garter snakes, and white-tailed deer; sixty miles of grassland shadowed by cumulus clouds and tended by innumerable hawks soaring high above prairie, watching me watch them, I suppose.

HEART

OF

THE

SANDHILLS

I leave Fort Robinson and drive east to Chadron, where I visit the state college, a local health food store, and then the city library, to browse history books. Late in the day I break a long tradition of avoiding bars and stop at the Cave, where I order a 7-Up. It is a fortuitous decision, since I meet a woman there who leaves me with a phrase and look that will guide me back into the hills and a deeper understanding of their contradictions. Her name is Rita, and she and her companion have been working on a pitcher of beer since long before I arrived. I take the stool next to her; she swirls my way and we are instantly into a conversation about the hills.

"It's the romance," she says, "the romance of the hills . . . especially in morning light when they're purple. . . ." Her hands pause in space and she gazes off over my shoulder. She does not finish the thought, but the expression on her face tells me what "romance" means—land so elegant, light so pristine that the whole image becomes this luscious moment for the senses, and for one flashing instant you believe you have witnessed something blessed. I have seen these hills when the light on the dunes turns grasses the color of lavender. Lakes reflect crystalline blue. Streaks of burgundy blanket a horizon of uninterrupted, undulating dunes, potent as a moment of silence. I have seen silence roll off in all directions in these hills—prairie so regal, so simple that the notion of romance rises like a heavy scent in morning.

And yet I have been in these hills when that same beauty, that same expanse of grass and sand and wind and sky, can do little more than drive me crazy. I cannot reach a town fast enough, enter a conversation swiftly enough. I cannot sup of the sustenance that comes from community deeply enough. I cannot—plain and simple—get out of these damn hills fast enough.

Perhaps it is their size that evokes such emotion in me. The Sandhills region fills the entire north-central part of Nebraska, twenty thousand square miles. I looked it up on the map once and figured Vermont and New Hampshire would fit into the hills, with space left over. Now imagine that space, Vermont and New Hampshire, without trees. There are some in the hills, along streams and rivers, in gullies and around towns—trees planted by man. There are even two manmade forests, totaling about twenty-five thousand acres—one in Cherry County and another covering portions of Thomas and Blaine counties—but these are not naturally occurring trees. The real Sandhills, the rangeland, the bulk of those twenty thousand square miles, is treeless: acre upon acre of treeless sandy hills covered with green and hazel-colored grasses.

Nebraska's Sandhills region is the largest sand sea in the western hemisphere. I like those words, "sand sea," because they really tell you what this place looks like: a vast expanse of ocean tossed with waves, except these waves are sand, and they're just not moving right now. This place I love is one of the largest sand dune regions in the world, and many people think it is the last true American prairie, because it is still intact. The tallgrass prairie that once covered Iowa, Illinois, Wisconsin, and Minnesota has for the most part been turned to cropland.

I spend the night at the Roundup Motel in Chadron, wake to a High Plains blue sky and a desire to move beyond memories, to move into current stories of the land. I drive east on Highway 20 and pass through Hay Springs and Rushville, places I have visited before. I am just miles from the town of Gordon, near the area where Nebraska writer Mari Sandoz grew up. Late in the 1800s her father, Jules Sandoz—the focus of her most famous book, *Old*

Jules—entertained Indians and pioneers alike in the hills near here. I am seduced by history and stop on the picturesque downtown street to make a photograph. A white Chevy ambles up Main, curves a wide U at the end of the street near the railroad tracks. I lower my camera to let the car pass. A man's face in the passenger window stares; his arm rises. He flips me the bird. The insult is one I cannot take lightly, and I instantly consider all sorts of sinister ways to repay his behavior in kind. I suppose any woman would be angry, and I suppose some women could brush it off. But I am not that kind of woman. I am a woman who was raped at the age of twenty-four by a stranger who tried to kill me, and every foray I make into the world is shaped by that experience. I have grown into the kind of woman who does not take kindly to men lording power over me. What keeps me from walking up and smashing my fist through his window I cannot say. Instead, I fume my way back to my car and for some reason drive west out of town, retracing my steps. In just miles, though, I whip the car around and head back toward Gordon. I intend to give him a piece of my mind, but there is a car approaching, and I recognize it as the white Chevy. It passes and I catch a glimpse of the slack face of the fat man in the pas-senger seat. I flip a U and follow, imagining I shoot out the tires of his car, *Thelma & Louise* style. I drive for miles trailing the white Chevy, dreaming my revenge—and I *am* dreaming. I know this on a conscious level. I am playing out my rage and anger, his act having tapped into a bottomless well of hatred. How does one come back from a violent act? How does one live again in the world of mundane, day-to-day events? I can tell you only how I came back: slowly. Piece by piece. Habit by habit, scratching back a life. There were no epiphanies; there have been no resolutions; it has been only the step-by-step reclaiming of a life once lived. I cannot tell you even today that I have resolved my feelings about near death and sexual assault. What I can say is that I have taken the power of my rage, and I have tried to redirect it; I have tried to focus it on speaking for those things I love; I have tried to transform anger into action.

I lose his car in Rushville and feel the need to get out and shake from my body the filth of his actions and the filth of my own anger.

I turn the car to the east again and plow back across prairie. I feel burned clean, even though I have done little but in my mind contort the possibilities, juggle the options, play out my passions, rediscover a reason to go on: You can have my innocence; you can have my trust; but you cannot have the things I love.

The water in these hills is inextricably linked to the Ogallala Aquifer, a huge underground water reserve, the largest in the West, stretching five hundred miles from Nebraska to Texas. Its deep end is centered right below the Sandhills. Water experts liken the Ogallala to a lake of very old, very pure water. They say it holds as much water as Lake Huron, and it is being pumped, pumped dry, perhaps.

The advent of irrigation on the Great Plains at mid-century, aided by center pivots—those spindly, self-propelled sprinklers on wheels—perpetuated the expansion of row crop agriculture as a viable source of income in an area long known to be arid. As more and more agricultural enterprises located on lands above the Ogallala Aquifer, farmers tapped the groundwater reserve to sustain their crops. In Nebraska alone over seventy percent of water used for irrigation is pumped from the aquifer. Already wells tapping the Ogallala in the Panhandle of Texas have gone dry, and water levels as far north as Kansas have been seriously depleted.

This ancient reserve of water, the Ogallala, sustains the ponds I see from tops of dunes across the hills. It percolates up through the soil, rising above the ground where the water table is high, forming marshes and lakes. It sustains consistent flows in four major Sandhills rivers—the Snake, Loup, Calamus, and Dismal, all of which have their headwaters in the hills—and it is the largest source of drinking water between Rapid City, South Dakota, and Lubbock, Texas.

Deep below the surface lie a collection of sandy soils called the Ogallala group, the source of this aquifer's name. Some twenty million years ago, sediment from mountains located in the areas we now call Colorado and Wyoming was washed eastward in ancient valleys and deposited on the Great Plains. Over millions of years it was covered by layer after layer of other kinds of sediment.

Over time, water percolated through the topsoil and became trapped in the sand and gravel of the Ogallala. It is held there by an impermeable layer of bedrock beneath this layer of sediment. Experts like to argue that the aquifer spills over into other geologic formations, and they recommend a different name: High Plains Aquifer. Still, Ogallala persists as the name most people give this water resource.

I met a man in Stapleton two weeks ago. He was elderly, and even in summer wore a hat and heavy jacket. We passed each other in the door of the post office and ended up in a conversation about the hills. He called the Ogallala Aquifer a heart; he said it was the "heart of the Sandhills." If it is the heart, then water is the blood, and those who pump the aquifer are bleeding it dry. Water is pumped in some places from the Ogallala Aquifer—by a centrifugal pump and motor—at a rate that lowers the water table five feet per year. The natural rate of replenishment averages a quarter inch per year. And all this to nourish crops that require more water than falls west of the hundredth meridian.

The hundredth is one of those ephemeral but nonetheless pivotal demarcation lines. Beyond the hundredth, the West begins: Rainfall levels dip below twenty inches a year, dry winds suck moisture from topsoil, the land becomes arid. The hundredth meridian cuts directly through Nebraska, near the eastern edge of the Sandhills, and agriculture mavens in Nebraska and across the Great Plains have known for decades that beyond the hundredth row crop agriculture is clinging to marginal land.

Some have even tried growing corn in the Sandhills, a truly foolish endeavor. Pesticides and fertilizer are carried directly through the porous, sandy soil and into the aquifer, fouling that pure water source. In addition, chemicals used to enhance crop yields run off into rivers and streams—a problem anywhere agriculture exists—and settle out into lakes and reservoirs, where the excess nutrients, from fertilizer, feed a burst of algae that degrades the aquatic environment. Pesticides settle into the sediment and ultimately work their way into the food chain. These are not new problems, but they are happening in Nebraska, in the Sandhills, in a place I love.

*   *   *

I have been driving east for miles now with the windows rolled down and the top open in my car. This prairie can heal you, and I let wind open my soul. Miles of grass and fences lined with sunflowers skim by. I pass a field filled with blue penstemon shimmering like a lake at high noon. I drive right through Gordon without even looking, and on east into rolling hills, hills that heave as if some force beneath the earth pushes at them, urging them to pitch hypnotically into shapes so subtle that mystery seems to rise from their essence. I get on track; this is a journey to the heart of the hills.

East of Gordon I pull into a roadside rest area and read a plaque that tells the history of ranching in the hills. It is the story of the Newman ranch. The year was 1879, a time when Nebraskans still kept to the edges of the uncharted hills. It had been a hard winter, the story goes, and Newman had lost a lot of cattle. In spring, he sent a party of cowhands south from his ranch into the hills to round up any Herefords that might have strayed and survived. What those cowhands found—vast expanses of prairie grass, streams and lakes pulsing with water, herds of fat stray cattle living off the land—changed this state forever. The Sandhills became known as prime rangeland, and cattlemen poured in with their herds.

It is most visibly the native grasses that blanket these hills that make it such good grazing land, but at heart it's the water. In fertile hay meadows, naturally irrigated by the aquifer, ranchers cut the native grass, or hay, in summer to feed their herds in winter, and water from the aquifer is released back to the surface and atmosphere during short-term droughts, keeping the grasses alive even when land outside the hills languishes for want of water. Naturally occurring lakes and ponds throughout the hills provide water for livestock. As a matter of fact, there are so many lakes in these hills, it's hard to keep track of them, partly because in some years water evaporates more quickly than it is replenished by rain, and borders between lakes and marshes fluctuate. On average, though, there are about two thousand lakes in Nebraska's Sandhills—not deep lakes, of course, not recreational skiing and boating lakes, but rather naturally subirrigated valleys, some of which hold water deep enough to qualify as ponds, and all of which enhance this place as ranchland. But more: They make it perfect habitat for birds, and the birds come in waves: white pelicans, grebes, loons, double-crested cormorants, bitterns, herons, egrets, trumpeter swans, geese, ducks, rails, American coots, sandhill cranes, plovers, killdeer, black-necked stilts, American avocets, spotted sandpipers, willets, snipes, phalaropes, terns. Dozens of species of birds not resident to these hills use prairie lakes on journeys north and south.

Something compels me to keep driving east on this highway. Perhaps it is the wind flushing through my car. I feel awake, directed. A kind of clarity comes into my mind that I have not felt yet on this journey. Ahead is the town of Cody. I drove through Cody weeks ago and wrote in my notes: "Little towns are depressing." I had been making my first broad sweeps through the hills, driving rapidly north and south, east and west, dipping into towns, then pushing back into prairie. In most towns grain elevators sat empty along railroad tracks. Storefronts gaped. Streets were dusty and little traveled.

The history of settlement in the Sandhills mirrors that of the entire western portion of the United States: a few years of intense optimism followed by decades of reality. Population in most Sandhills towns peaked in the 1920s and has been in a steady decline ever since. Some towns, like Hoagland and Antioch, have ceased to exist. Other outposts, like Seneca and Gandy, once destined in the minds of promoters to become thriving hubs, are now a string of boarded-up buildings. If lucky, they retain a post office and maybe a grocery.

After the Civil War, as the transcontinental railroad pushed west across Nebraska, hopeful immigrants poured into the state. Encouraged by an era of remarkable rainfall never seen again—records topped forty inches annually in the late 1880s—they moved plows into the Sandhills, founded communities, and awaited a branch line of the railroad. If the town failed to receive tracks, it died; locals moved to a more promising village.

Once again I am drawn north off the highway into Cody. It is late afternoon and hot. The temperature has been near one hundred degrees all day. In the park the sprinklers are running. The grass is thick, damp, and green. I stop in the shade and walk straight into the arching jets of water. Water pelts my chest, and I double up with laughter, then turn, swirl and pirouette through the spray. Grass squishes between my bare toes. The town appears deserted, although the front door of the gas station across the street sits open wide. No one comes out to watch me, though. No cars move down Main Street. No one exits or enters the grocery. I play until I am soaked, then rest on a white picnic table bench and let the warm south wind dry my clothes. On the edge of town as I drive out to meet the highway, I catch sight of a sign: "Cody: A Town Too Tough to Die."

The Sandhills communities that survive today are blessed with a rail line or major highway, county courthouse, regional hospital, or consolidated school, although those that have linked the local economy to the railroad now face the drying up of that last life-giving artery as financially troubled companies pull lines from Sandhills outposts, abandoning tracks and towns as they go.

The importance of the railroad in the Sandhills is reflected in the most basic of elements—the layout of the town. Nearly every Sandhills town follows a similar design: Where the tracks enter city limits, there sits a huddle of grain elevators and cattle loading docks, the latter falling down, boards weathered gray by wind and rain. Since trucking cattle to market supplanted the boxcar, this part of the rail business has disappeared. Branching from the rail hub will be a grid of streets: downtown, with one wide main street running at a ninety-degree angle from the tracks. Businesses line Main Street. Homes fall away from the main drag on streets with names like Elm, Willow, Locust, and Cedar, hopeful invocations of permanence and comfort.

Most towns are located on rivers, since these were the first and only places travelers could get water to sustain the lives of their animals and families. The first trails followed rivers; railroads followed trails; highways followed railroads—a pattern of settlement and decay that has defined these hills.

It is early evening when I reach Nenzel. I am less than half an hour away from Valentine, where I will spend the night, and I am eager to get to a motel. Still, I pull off and cruise into town. A short row of storefronts on Main Street is Nenzel. At the end sits the post office, a frame shelter built over a collection of mailboxes. The open side faces south, the covered side north. One business in town sells groceries, mostly to people camping and fishing in the national forest ten miles south. Nenzel is a town whose best days, like Ericson's, are part of the past. I flip a U and head back to Highway 20. The sunlight is warm, golden, and low on the horizon. It glances off windshields and reflects from the windows of a white frame building. The buzzing of cicadas fills the air, and I slow as I drive past Nenzel's block of abandoned storefronts. One catches my eye. Despite peeling paint and an almost invisible name stenciled above the door, Dick's Bar is open. One man sits at the counter, his frame silhouetted by sunlight streaming in an interior window. A lone beer light flickers: Coors.

In thirty minutes I am in Valentine. I cruise the motels and check in at the Dunes, a tidy place with a distinct air of the 1960s. The decor makes me feel as if George Jetson might walk out of the bathroom any minute. I shower, change clothes, and head downtown.

The first time I passed through Valentine this summer, government subsidy checks had just been distributed on the Rosebud Indian Reservation directly north in South Dakota, and Native Americans with too much liquor sagged in doorways and shared bottles on stair steps. The town had a sad look, but tonight I am struck by the vitality of Valentine. Main Street is wide and clean and lined with cars and pickups. Store windows are full of merchandise. Businesses fan out from the central artery; many—a lumberyard, a grocery store, an appliance repair shop, a car dealership—occupy side streets. There are two newspapers, a dozen eating establishments, a discount store on the edge of town, even fast food and quick gas shops.

On Main Street there is a huge heart-shaped sign above one business: "Valentine's," it announces. Through the double windows track lighting shines down on a Native American headdress. Walls are lined with black-and-white photographs. Glass cases fill the middle of the room. Inside the art gallery I talk with the owner, David, and a local artist, Mark, about the Niobrara and its pending designation as a scenic river. The Niobrara has long been recognized as a treasure in Nebraska. It flows undammed for most of its length across the state—four-hundred-plus miles—and the valley of the Niobrara near Valentine has earned the title of biological crossroads of the nation. Six distinct vegetation types converge here, and the banks of the river host numerous plants and animals at the outermost edges of their range. For years this area was threatened by a proposed project called the Norden Dam, but that plan, which would have dammed the Niobrara and flooded this unique ecological niche, seems dead now. Scenic designation arrives as a viable way to protect this area.

David is convinced Valentine is destined to become a tourist haven. Already hundreds flock to Valentine each summer to canoe the Niobrara. "Just think what will happen when the river has national scenic designation," he says. Mark fills me in on the background: While some locals see the designation as a boon to the economy, area ranchers see it as a threat to their independence. They don't believe the government can better manage their river-abutting land.

Inside a glass display case, I see two eagle-feather fans. "They're made by Sioux friends on the Rosebud," David says. I tell him the gallery reminds me of one I might see in Santa Fe, and he beams at the mention of that place. I walk around studying Mark's photographs. They capture the light on the Sandhills and on the Niobrara River landscape, evoking the sense of a place as yet wild and untrammeled.

Mark offers to show me Fort Falls at the Fort Niobrara National

Wildlife Refuge the next day, and we agree to meet in the morning. I bid my new friends farewell and walk across the street to the Peppermill Restaurant. Country music rises from a cedar-fenced beer garden, and a raft of Ford pickups line the street around the restaurant.

The next day we drive Highway 12 east to the refuge, where we climb down into a small canyon. The sound of falling water drowns our words. Fort Falls is a pristine, spring-fed waterfall flowing into the Niobrara. The smell is damp, and we are the only people there as morning light illuminates the water and walls of the canyon. Leaving the refuge, we pass a fleet of road graders that hack at the landscape, widening the road and putting in a perfectly angled off-ramp to the Niobrara River.

In town we wave good-bye, and I visit the historical museum, a one-story brick building with many rooms of displays. I move slowly through the reconstructed pioneer settings, reflecting on the nature of settlement and progress. The ranchers who came to these hills in the 1800s pushed from the land the Native Americans who lived here, erased from history their way of life. Will the next wave of progress push from the hills the very ranchers who once claimed this land as their own? Will scenic river designation launch a new wave of exploration, a wave of urban souls seeking a piece of the wild? It is possible, you know. Open space and cheap housing abound here, and there is only one Boulder, one Moab, and one Santa Fe. When all the obvious places are gentrified, will people turn to these hills? Will the declining life of ranching in the hills, a life lived on the land, shift into an economy dominated by tourism, as in so many of the last untrammeled rural places in the American West?

It is late afternoon when I drive south out of Valentine. This land is a jumble of contradictions. High atop dunes, prairie appears dry. Yucca plants spike the horizon. Here grassland birds such as meadowlarks and hawks make their home, but deep in the next valley, wetland plants flank marshes; a placid bed of water covers the ground, and shorebirds feed.

I don't know why I turn off the highway when I do. I have no particular destination; it is just a sense that tells me this is the next place to go, a sense that down this road lies knowledge that will move me closer to an understanding of this region, closer to the things I need to say. Yellow light slants in from the west. The prairie I cross is flat and wet. Ponds dot fields. Directly south of the narrow road rises a huge dune that juts from the horizon like the side of a building, climbing perhaps three hundred feet. The sun's rays reflect from browned grasses growing on its side, and the dune seems to shimmer. It appears warm and sensuous, round and full of light. I climb to the top of my car to make a photograph and recognize a familiar pattern: These hills cannot be captured with one image. I must make a series of photographs that form a one-hundred-and-eighty-degree panorama.

The Sandhills rise from ancient landscape. One hundred million years ago an inland sea retreated and wind and water began their work. Experts disagree about the dunes, though. Some say they are twenty thousand years old. Others insist they are younger, a mere eight thousand years. One thing scientists do agree on is an elaborate classification system for shapes the dunes take. A barchan is a crescent-shaped dune with the ends pointing downwind; a barchanoid ridge is a row of connected barchans. The barchanoid ridge is the most common dune formation in the hills, covering close to five thousand square miles and yielding the tallest of the dunes, which is in Grant County: four hundred and forty-four feet from base to ridge. There are parabolic dunes, which are U-shaped. And linear dunes, with row after row of parallel ridges. Domelike dunes are circular mounds, and domal ridges occur when mounds connect and form a row.

As I move my camera, capturing images, I reflect on the stunning rate at which this landscape could be transformed. Recent research suggests that global warming, the next major drought, a falling water table—any major and prolonged shift in the ecosystem—could send these dunes wandering. In terms of geologic time, this manifestation of the dunes is a passing phase.

Framing the last image, I see dust rising in the distance. Cattle are moving toward me, filling this tiny road from fence line to fence line. A car engine would spook these animals, so I sit silently on the hood, load my camera, and wait as the herd picks up speed. One man on horseback and a companion in a pickup truck push the cattle forward. Through a telephoto lens I am being overrun by white-faced Herefords. They stop right in front of my car, bawling. The horseman urges them on.

"Shootin' a movie?" he calls.

"Just making some photos," I return.

He drives the cattle past. Their warm bodies brush my legs; they flow like water around my car. The pickup pulls up. He wants to know what part of Iowa I'm from. License plates don't explain complexities. I make it simple.

"Eastern edge."

"Where 'bouts? My mom's from over there. Been back there myself."

I tell him I grew up in Nebraska.

"What part?"

"Polk County."

"Yep, I been there."

There is a slightly awkward but friendly pause. He dips his hat. "Well, I oughta get along up there and help with them cows."

We nod.

With the cattle behind me, I start the car and move on. Less than a mile ahead the road loses pavement, turns to gravel. A ranch stands nearby. Behind it stretches a shallow expanse of water the color of royal velvet. Red-winged blackbirds cry from cattail stalks in a marsh across the road. Over the hill golden light reflects from a broad, flat lake. Red Angus cattle raise their heads and stare.

Most ranchers in this region run what's called a cow-calf operation, which means they own cows that produce calves, usually in late winter or early spring. The cow-calf unit is kept on the range until calves are weaned and sold in the fall, although some ranchers keep calves over for a second season of grazing, trucking them to sale barns the following year, where they are auctioned off to feedlots. There they spend their last days fattening on grain.

Because of the uncertainty of ranching—high-priced land, unpredictable weather, and unstable cattle prices—many family enterprises have been sold to larger concerns, corporations that in the 1970s and early 1980s bought thousands of acres of rangeland in the hills, then turned around and hired locals to work the operation, for a wage. Selling out was the only answer for some ranchers who couldn't turn a profit from raising cattle and whose children were not returning to take over the family ranch.

I follow the threadlike road from pavement to gravel to sand until it intersects a highway, which must be 97 south of Valentine. I drive a few miles, then leave the main road again, turning onto another partially paved back trail indicated on the state map as a thin gray line, a line that to me speaks of adventure. If all goes well, I should end up in the village of Brownlee.

Even as late as the 1920s, highways in Nebraska skirted the Sandhills. What roads did exist were sandy wagon trails that followed valleys, crossing hills at low points. They were crooked, winding roads with many cattle gates that existed primarily to serve local traffic and often dead-ended at ranches. In 1916 the Federal-Aid Highway Act encouraged Nebraska's legislature to organize the building of highways, but the plans they made essentially ignored the hills: The Blue Pole Road followed the northern border, and the Lincoln Highway edged the south. The only highway they planned that would enter the hills was the Potash Highway, which was scheduled to run from Grand Island to Alliance, almost three hundred miles. It was named for the potash plants near Antioch, east of Alliance, and is now known as Highway 2. In 1932 the Potash Highway became the first paved road to pierce the heart of the hills, but pavement, of course, was nothing like we know today. Because both clay and gravel, favored paving materials in those days, were scarce in the hills, oil gained popularity. Oil was laid onto a sand trail, coating it about five inches deep, which created a somewhat acceptable surface. The Potash Highway when completed was a patchwork of clay, gravel, and oil. It must have seemed like a freeway back then.

World War II slowed road work in the hills, but by the 1950s several U.S. highways bisected the area. It was not until 1972, though, that a north-south route was completed in the far western part of Cherry County, a county larger than the state of Connecticut: Highway 61, which joins Hyannis and Merriman, an epic road, sixty-seven miles long, which, when completed, cut in half travel time between the southern and northern borders of the county.

A few miles into my journey toward Brownlee I see a car approach. It is a Mustang, 1970s vintage, and inside a young man with a crew cut makes tracks for Highway 97. I wonder if he lives at one of the ranches on this road, a road that meanders thirty to forty miles into ranch land with no towns along the way except for the hamlet of Brownlee at the far end of the road, a town for which the map lists no population.

I am reminded of a young woman I met at the Arthur Bowring State Historical Park, a working ranch north of Merriman. She was a student at Chadron State College, working at the ranch for the summer, and she gracefully showed me around the grounds, reciting stories of Eve Bowring's life and her own. I remember one thing she said. When I asked about her plans after college, she responded quickly, "Oh, I plan to get out of here. There's nothing to do."

I wonder if this young man in the Mustang is anxiously escaping chores at a family ranch, awaiting the day he will graduate from high school and leave the hills. Few young people return anymore, a trend reflected in towns. Churches serve elderly populations; school enrollments shrink. Settlement in the Sandhills is drying up and has been for decades. What is to become of this place? When the elders who run the ranches pass on, what will happen to this tradition of ranching in the hills?

A rain shower breaks out. Thunder rumbles over the dunes, and white spikes of lightning drill toward earth. In Brownlee the rain has just stopped. Puddles reflect the rose-colored light of a clearing sky. The North Loup River surges through town, lapping at the underside of a low bridge. Here is one of the clearest manifestations of the contradictions of this land: There appears to be so much water. How could it be threatened? There are those among the water experts who argue that aquifer recharge rates are high in the hills—the soil is porous; little precipitation runs off—that current pumping has not affected water levels, that rain and snowmelt will sustain this abundant Sandhills resource. Others, however, point to profligate use elsewhere on the Great Plains, from South Dakota and Wyoming through Nebraska, Colorado, Kansas, Oklahoma, and into Texas. They remind us that the aquifer is one system and that overuse in one area will adversely affect another.

I cannot prove that this view of the aquifer as an interwoven system is the right view; I can not prove that pumping elsewhere on the Great Plains above the Ogallala Aquifer will affect water levels in the Sandhills, and yet I cannot prove it will not. In the Pacific Northwest, where I live now, people once thought the big trees would last forever. There were so many of them; how could they ever run out? And so they cut and cut and cut. Today there are only pockets of old growth.

There must be some thoughtful approach in the future to the use of the waters of the Ogallala Aquifer; there must be some thoughtful approach to crop choices. It may make sense to the economy of Nebraska to grow corn in prairie, but does it make environmental sense to grow corn, an oasis crop, in arid land where water must be pumped to sustain its growth?

Night is pushing in and I must find a place to stay. Once Brownlee was a thriving town. People came here from miles in every direction. A stage stopped here, and there were stables, a hotel, and a general store. I take a picture of the small frame building that houses the post office. There are two churches in town and a community hall, all still used, but there are no other services. In Thedford the Arrowhead Motel is full. The closest town with a room is Halsey, fifteen miles east, but when I arrive, the Keeney Stockade is full, too. It is past ten o'clock, and I know the closest towns with motels are Broken Bow and Burwell, each sixty miles away. I drive east out of town on the Potash Highway.

Somewhere in prairie I find myself watching the northern sky and wondering what town I see out there, lights warming the horizon, but there is no town. There is no town of any size that could cast such a hue into the night between here and Sioux Falls, South

Dakota, three hundred miles north and east. I pull to the side of the road. The night is black. Stars cover earth's dome; there is no moon. On the horizon pulsate beams of light, greenish, then red. It is like a huge light show without music, no sound at all except the wind in my ears. I realize I am witnessing the northern lights, the aurora borealis, and for one flashing moment I feel supreme connectedness, as if I could reach out and touch the North Pole, as if everything in between were related.

It is heresy, you know, for me to suggest the planting of crops other than corn in Nebraska, a state that has built its economy around that crop. The little towns that still, exist support farmers who grow corn. Ranchers in the Sandhills sell their cattle to feedlots, where they are fattened on corn. These feedlots have become primary sources of employment in towns across the Plains, towns struggling to stay alive, and yet standing here watching these fingers of light bend around the planet to meet my eyes, I cannot escape the notion that all parts of this system are connected. I do not think it is ridiculous to believe that excessive pumping of water in other Great Plains states can ultimately affect water levels in the Sandhills.

At some point in the dark night pummeling across prairie, I give up the search for a motel. The Big Six beckons. It has been several years since I was in Ericson and in the Big Six, but still I drive all the way there, even though I don't arrive until well after midnight. My father opened the cabin earlier in the summer, and so I have little to do but unlock doors and open windows. I rummage in the linen closet for the oldest and most worn set of sheets, make up my bunk in the bedroom of my childhood, then slide between layers of softened cotton. Memories of family swirl around me, voices and laughter, ghosts of summer evenings and sounds of the prairie. Outside the window, above the raised bangboard, cottonwood leaves flutter lightly, and beyond, pitch-colored sky and swirling heavens fill the night. When I am lost or wandering, the Big Six always calls to me, like a voice of reason. Here I find a place of calm, a place of known smells, of familiar furnishings. I pad out for a final glass of water. It is cold and refreshes, and I know, most decidedly, that I am home.

The next day I drive into town. Just as I reach the stop sign on Main Street, a pig dashes by. Right behind this animal run three men, arms flailing; a hat flies to the ground. Classic Ericson. Some things never change. The Fourth of July is about a week away, and so I assume this pig has something to do with that celebration. Of course, that may not be the case. There's a wagon that sits on top of the Hungry Horse. It looks like planned decor, but it isn't. It just appeared one night. So there's no telling what this pig may mean. I stop at the Hungry Horse to visit. No one seems surprised to see me; I slide in with the regulars at the bar, and a friend offers me a beer. "Got work to do," I say. "I'll just take a Coke." I spend the next hour catching up with my friends, but never quite unearthing the source and meaning of the pig.

Later in the week I am invited to visit probably the largest cattle-feeding operation in the hills, located near Bartlett. Around Ericson they just call it Foxley's. The place is also known as the Thunderbolt Ranch. It's owned by William Foxley, one of the biggest cattle feeders in the country. While once I preferred to avoid this side of Nebraska, I now want to know the specifics of agriculture in the hills, and so I accept the invitation.

Foxley's covers about twelve thousand acres, with center pivots irrigating almost six thousand acres of corn. When harvested, the corn is milled right there on the property into feed for the cattle. During my visit Foxley was running sixty-five thousand head of cattle, with plans to bring in another ten thousand in July. These cattle are confined to pens in metal barns, each half a mile long. Eighteen pens make up each barn, and each pen holds between two hundred and two hundred and fifty cows, body to body. The cows are fed around the clock. They have nothing to do but eat. After about one hundred and eighty days they are sold to slaughterhouses.

There are a number of insults to Sandhills life embodied in an operation like Foxley's, the most serious of which is the actual plowing of the Sandhills. This is fragile land stabilized by the native grasses. When the sand is exposed, it blows away, as ranchers learned in the 1930s, when overgrazing damaged the roots of plants, and vast sections of prairie went bald. It took years of careful management to bring back the mantle of grasses that now blanket the hills. In addition, once the thin layer of topsoil in the Sandhills is turned and the wind carries it away, excessive amounts of fertilizer are required to grow corn in these hills. Fertilizer is easily carried into the water table, moving through the porous, sandy soil with water pumped from the aquifer and used to irrigate the crop. Furthermore, while pumped water from the aquifer can sustain corn in semi-arid prairie, the heavy extraction required to irrigate an operation of this size lowers levels in area drinking wells and, by drawing down the water table, alters the effects of natural subirrigation in neighboring meadows.

Despite these problems, some believe operations like Foxley's are the future of the Sandhills. Ranchers pasturing cattle can hardly turn a profit, and corn increases earnings from a piece of prairie. They forget, though, that the water is a limited resource.

One would think that being back in Ericson after such an absence would be plenty of reason to remember every moment of my stay. On the contrary, though, I am having trouble remembering the details of that Fourth of July. Only one image rises. I am sitting at the long table on the screened porch of the Big Six Country Club with my father. We are eating dinner, chatting and laughing, enjoying each other's intelligence and wit. It is a rare and sweet moment. Like the Sandhills, my family is a study in contrasts, appearing one day to be one thing, around the corner revealing a different face.

After my mother left, difficult and awkward times befell the remnant of my family. My brother limped off to college; my father and I stumbled out of sync, rubbing each other the wrong way and crawling off to separate corners to lick our wounds. From this private, independent tendency grew a tradition of separateness, and perhaps even blame, he blaming me as a woman for my mother's departure, me blaming him as a man for letting her go. We argued often. Today, though, we find a happy space as father and daughter, pushing beyond our separateness, discovering that despite our differences we are intricately linked.

There is much to be learned from a land of contradictions like the Sandhills. Species that in other settings would be separated by landscape, each dependent on a single, specific environment— prairie, wetland—are brought together here, creating a rich, interdependent world defined by those differences. My family, like this commingling of wetland life and prairie life, is a meeting of opposites that on the surface appear dramatically different. A longer view shows our intricate dependency. Even though we are a family broken apart, we are a family still. Even though by separation we have grown into firmly etched individuals, we are joined by history, by land, and by love. Like the plants and animals of the Sandhills, we coexist in different worlds, side by side.

There is one more place I feel drawn to in the hills, one last place I need to see before I return to Iowa: the Crescent Lake National Wildlife Refuge in Garden County, a place set aside solely for the honoring of eared grebes, pronghorn antelope, sharp-tailed grouse, tiger salamanders, a place set aside for the protection of all the creatures of this prairie, a place unmistakably dependent on the rich supply of groundwater.

I leave Ericson and the Big Six late on a smoldering afternoon in July, sometime after my birthday, and drive west on a journey that will take me through many of the places we traveled as a family when I was a child, places that evoke memories of a life long past. It seems a fitting way to wind up a trip to the hills, and I embark ready to greet the stories that will rise.

In Burwell I stop for dinner at the drive-in. Burwell is home to Nebraska's Big Rodeo, held annually about this time of year. As children we never missed the carnival of spinning rides. We ate sloppy joes at the church lunch counter, then climbed the wooden bleachers and watched quarter horses cut cloverleaf patterns around barrels. In the arena, cowboys with kerchiefs flapping from necks soared from humps of Brahma bulls and backs of bucking horses. Later, in the fairway, my father steered me toward a carnival wagon lined with glass cases, each filled with trinkets and a miniature crane with an arm, chain, and bucket. He worked the handle again and again, dropping quarters into the machine, until he had successfully positioned the scoop over some treasure, lifted it, and dumped it into the chute that would send it out and into my hands.

Sixty miles of empty highway link me with Dunning, where I merge with the Potash Highway and follow the Middle Loup River west. Outside Halsey I detour south into the Nebraska National Forest and drive slowly through towering pines, remembering an earlier journey when my family pulled off the highway into this forest. The trees were small and planted in exact rows. We climbed from the station wagon and my father swept his arms through the air, gesturing toward the seedlings. "Someday this forest will be big trees." I recall looking across the tops of the tiny trees into prairie beyond and trying to imagine this possibility.

In Thedford I check in at the Arrowhead Motel. In the room the bulb of a small lamp reveals a panoramic view printed on the shade: Hereford cattle, sandy hills, a cowpoke on horseback, a corral. I give the shade a push and it spins on the finial. Around and around the image goes: corral, cattle, hills, cowpoke, corral, cattle, hills, cowpoke. I push open a small window above the bed. Cattle bawl in the distance. The low rumble of a train drifts in. Coyotes howl. The moon is big, round, and yellow, and makes the sky look midnight blue around the edges. I smell a feedlot somewhere out there in the night.

The next morning I stop in Mullen at the newspaper office and buy a copy of the county newspaper. I spot an Apple Macintosh computer in the composing area. Yes, the woman behind the counter tells me, the newspaper has graduated to desktop publishing, but their press is in North Platte, seventy-five miles south. She says out-county news is phoned in. Some correspondents compile the neighborly visits and dinners, homecomings and gossip, and mail in their reports. In the *Hooker County Tribune* there are grocery store ads, announcements of anniversaries, deaths, births, a long list of speeding tickets, and an entire section heralding the benefits of beef.

As I approach Hyannis, my parents' words come back from decades before: "More millionaires per capita than anywhere else in the country," they said about this place. Big ranches, steady cattle prices, predictable rainfall: They all contributed to the wealth—or myth. If it ever really existed, though, it certainly doesn't anymore. In town, on the corner of the highway and Main Street, rests the ancient Hotel Hyannis, a building listed on the National Historic Register as the only example of French Second Empire architecture in the Sandhills. Now it is a frowzy-looking place with a tattered barroom joined to a restaurant by a set of swinging doors. The real business is at the shiny new Amoco station right behind the hotel, where cars with license plates from Texas, South Dakota, Colorado, and Nebraska scoot in for gas and a quart soft drink. They scoot right out again, too, and zip out of town on Highway 2, the only east-west highway in this territory for fifty miles in any direction.

I decide to slow down and explore Hyannis. A sign in a small grocery advertises deli sandwiches—"For Lunch or Parties"—and I buy a deli roast beef, chips, and soda. At the top of the hill and the end of Main Street sit a small parking lot and a couple of picnic tables under huge cottonwoods on the lawn of the village library. I unpack my lunch and survey the town: a dozen streets crisscrossing this dune, each with a few frame houses facing the street, a grocery, post office, feed and hardware store, the Hotel Hyannis, Amoco station, and railroad line at the bottom of the hill, where trains shoot through town. Most cars on the streets are 1980s vintage Chevys, but right now there's not much movement in town. That may be why I hear the plaintive tune that rises on wind, carried to my ears from some house near this green. Floating above Hyannis is the melody of the one piano duet all children learned in the 1960s: "Heart and Soul." The lone notes float into air and fade.

Outside Mullen, near Ashby, I turn south onto the trail that will take me into the Crescent Lake National Wildlife Refuge. It is little more than a ranch road, one lane weaving across prairie. I crawl down its miles, soaking up the sound of meadowlarks and the vistas of clouds, dunes, and grass. Forty miles later I am lost somewhere in Garden County. My car climbs up and out of rolling hills onto a flat plain like that of eastern Nebraska. I decide I have slipped out of the Sandhills. They have eluded me. Here roads fall into one-mile grids—so unlike the hills. I assume I am south of the refuge and turn north every chance I get. Slowly the road shifts from gravel to narrow dirt to deep sand, then finally to ancient, broken asphalt. Far out in the west sheets of blinding light sparkle like pieces of a broken mirror: Crescent Lake, Blue Lake, Swan, then Island, Wolf, Alkali, Ashburger, Merrill, Goose Lake, Wild-horse, Schoonover—dozens of intertwined bodies of water surrounded with marshes, thick with birds. Water everywhere. This county is so fertile, so rich, that no word but "Garden" can suffice to describe it. I drive slowly, stopping often to walk trails into fields, listening to the quiet of land where no people live. Several deer graze in a damp pasture between lakes. Birdsong rises from water, like music.

Here in Garden County a wonderland of lakes stretches to the horizon. On the surface that place is protected as the Crescent Lake National Wildlife Refuge, but the element that keeps it vital is groundwater, a resource in these hills directly connected to the five-hundred-mile network of water-bearing sediments in the Ogallala Aquifer, which is not protected. More than any other part of the hydrologic cycle in these hills, the Ogallala shapes the nature of Sandhills life, and the water in that aquifer is finite—a fact myth-makers in the American West would prefer to ignore.

Today, spinning through sand, looking for the Crescent Lake National Wildlife Refuge, trekking outback in Grant and Garden counties, I found something not even the official state map would have you know exists: a secluded backcountry of rolling prairie veined with one-lane sand roads snaking over hills, and leading to towns twenty and thirty miles away; a whole community of ranches, of neighbors, spread across the land, invisible from the road, known only by hand-painted signs pointing down long ranch roads; a rich, interdependent web of life, days from any city, linked by spirit yet separated by miles of sand and wind. A church. A country school.

A grange hall. It was an unexpected gift, a mirror of the Sandhills: a place of surprising treasures, a life of values from another time— land, family, the natural world. It was the kind of discovery that in the fleeting movement of an eye can evoke a sense of gratitude so deep, so sharp, it catches in the throat like frozen winter wind. Gratitude nipped by sadness, because I know this place of southwest winds, of sand and water, of prairie junegrass and Hayden's penstemon, of hawks and great blue herons, of cottonwoods and dragonflies, of ranching, ritual, and tradition is threatened. Someday the water will run out.

$\mathcal{E}$PILOGUE

Five years have passed since my last journey to the heart of the Sandhills. I write to you today from my home on the Oregon coast. This place where I live is so much like the Sandhills that on some days I can convince myself I am in those sandy dunes of western Nebraska. Outside my house stretches an expanse of hummocky dunes covered with fluid beach grass. It spins and waves in the wind, making the dunes look alive, like the Sandhills in summer morning light. Shore pines dot the hollows of these dunes, like cedars in the hills—the green of these trees leaning more toward a yellow-green, though, than the blue-green of Sandhills cedars. Still, the contrast in color and texture between grass and tree is so similar I can fool myself while gazing out this picture window and into dunes. The sand spit where this house sits stretches for five miles south of here. At dusk I ride my bike into those unpopulated dunes. Their pitch and angle, the color of light on beach grass, is so like the look of the Sandhills, so like the mood of prairie before night, that I am momentarily transported. Some of the highest dunes that cascade down to Pacific beaches could pass exactly for a Sandhills dune. I am easily seduced by this landscape, drawn into remembrances of the hills. It is a curious twist of fate that has brought me to this house on the edge of the ocean in a land of sand and grass and wind to write this book. This place is so much like the Sandhills, and so much like Cape Cod, the one other place I have lived that captured my soul. It was inevitable, I suppose, that I would end up again in a place that reminds me of a sea of sand, of grassland.

I have not been in Ericson since 1993, when my husband and I stopped there on our move west to Oregon. All the old landmarks are still intact. Sandcrest, Honey's cabin, with my signature and the date I finished painting it, is still there, although it's not in the family anymore. It was sold about six years ago, but several years before that, Honey stopped going to the lake. She could no longer handle the drive. Just last year her house in Osceola was sold, and now she lives in a room at the Good Samaritan Center, at the foot of the hill we called the Ridge in Osceola, not far from my father's house. He checks on her daily. Sometimes she is spunky and knows him. Other times she is lost in song. "Such a loss," he said to me one time, and in his eyes I thought I could see reflections of Lake Ericson, of fishing and laughter-filled gatherings around the plank table. My grandfather Pop died so many years ago, I can hardly remember now what life was like with him. The passing of my grandparents and the loss of Sandcrest ball into a great weight in my chest, like the stone of a cherry sinking into my stomach.

Ruthie and David Gardner's place, near Sandcrest, was abandoned the last time I saw it. The dam, the old beach, the point, and Cram's cabin, where the swinging bridge once stood—they're all still part of the landscape, but other things have changed. A new wave of popularity has hit the lake, fueled by the completion of a reservoir on the Calamus River about thirty miles west of Ericson, a reservoir that sprawls across parts of Garfield and Loup counties. When that dam was completed and water began to back up on the river, flooding sandy prairie, lots were plotted and sold along the reservoir. Many realized that a cabin at cozy Lake Ericson, with its towering cottonwoods, was more pleasant and less expensive than a new place at the Calamus, and many decided the commute with power boat or fishing rods was not so bad. About that same time Loup Valley Rural Public Power District decided it no longer wanted to be responsible for management of Lake Ericson, and it pulled out. Locals tended the dam but realized the place would fall to ruin if something were not done. A Lake Association was formed that charged property owners dues, raising money to tend to lake business. Unfortunately, concurrent with these two events has come an insidious tendency toward suburbanization. Many of the old cabins have been remodeled into suburban-looking tract houses, and some have been turned into middle-class palaces with vaulted ceilings and tasteful patios. The most disturbing change, though, is the move to annihilate every open patch of prairie left. Split-rail fences have become the thing at Ericson and now everyone has fenced off their portion of grassland, which they regularly mow—an assault against the wild side of the lake. It is a sad and unmistakably mixed-up move when people believe that domesticating every corner of the earth is better for the land and for the people than allowing it to be what it is. Learning to inhabit wild places and allowing them to continue as wild places is an art few have learned, and so the end result is a Lake Ericson pleasantly cut up into fenced yards with proper homes. Weeds are frowned upon, and leaves that fall are swiftly raked and disposed. Cabins are decorated to look like houses in the city, and the flavor of a once-wild place clinging to the edge of the vast, uncharted Sandhills is rapidly being dulled.

My brother, Billy, is spending time at the Big Six these days, using that family haven as a place to regain a footing in the world, as each of us have done in our own time. We talked by phone the other night, and he said something that had never occurred to me—about the Big Six, about how it has filled over the years with such an odd assortment of trinkets. "You know, it's really like a *cabin* should be," Billy said. "Some of those new places . . . they aren't cabins at all."

He was right. The Big Six is a collection of mementos from seasons past: old hats, prizes won at rodeos, framed notices of rewards for captured gunslingers, fishing gear, tacky ashtrays, battered wind socks, chipped coffee cups, glowing beer signs, birds' nests, driftwood, and broken wind chimes. Layer upon layer of junk, each item a story unto itself. This is the shape of a real cabin, a place where family repairs to live an easier life, a life away from city concerns, a place where stories fill rooms. For the first time I realized the kind of gift that old cabin is to me. In it reside the stories of my life. Each room houses books and toys, paintings and rocks that someone can turn to and recite the legacy of family interaction. Even my mother's stories still fill these rooms: the round coffee table she painted in her trademark style, with compass directions for north, south, east and west, sits in front of the couches; my father's initials, which she carved into the wooden pillar that rises from the breakfast bar, blaze out over the kitchen; the hex sign she painted on the outside of the cabin to ward off evil spirits survives. When a small addition to the cabin threatened to eliminate the hex sign, my father sawed it out, mounted it on another board, and nailed it to the outer wall of the completed structure. Every few years Billy retouches the paint.

Recently, Billy told me that Mom had made for him a Pirates flag, which he flew regularly from the window of his apartment in Manhattan. When he traveled to the hills this fall, he carried it with him, and once my father left the Big Six and drove back to Osceola, Billy discreetly lowered the American flag that waves above the Big Six when my father is there and raised—thank God!—the Pirates flag, reasserting our hold on this piece of land, on this life in the hills.

Together, Billy and I own one of the prime pieces of undeveloped lakefront property—land my father bought years ago and gave to us a few years back, splitting evenly two ways. It is located along the northern leg of the lake, the portion that has turned now to luscious marsh, on land where Cram's cabin stands between the slough and lake. We keep it open, the grass unmown. A neighbor complains that it should be controlled, made to look tidy, but we assure her it is being just what it was meant to be—prairie, thank you—and it will stay that way. Her boyfriend took to parking his land-moving equipment on our prairie, driving concentric circles over the grass, flattening it, and I hate to admit it, but I had to call a surveyor and get him to put in stakes at the corners of the property, to send a message: We will not have the things we love destroyed. All those around us can shift to the blazing security of sodium vapor yard lights and neatly coiffed lawns, but we, the Pirate Nortons, will resist. We will keep a spot of wildness in the heart of this suburban plot.

Many of my old friends still live around Ericson and the Lake, but some have moved on and some have died. Shortly after my 1984 sojourn in the hills, Craig Spilinek was diagnosed with cancer. He was only in his early twenties. Right up to the end he remained friendly, magnanimous, a hearty spirit. It seems impossible to believe that that scrawny, inquisitive kid who came to my door visiting, who grew into a man who shared his friendship and kindness with me, is gone. I don't accept the fact very well. His parents, Bob and Teddi, still live at the Lake, but he was their only child, and his loss took a lot out of them. There are many in the hills who have lost their young to alcohol and accidents. With so few people living in this prairie land, each loss seems to ricochet through the hills, gaining momentum and weight as news spreads, pulling down the place as one large community. Land and family are what these ranchers and Sandhills folk have, and when they lose one or the other, the community of the hills feels the pain.

Dick and Bonnadel Foster continue to live on their place along the River Road leading into town from Lake Ericson. I spoke with them recently by phone; they listened patiently as I read portions of my book, then politely corrected my mistakes and confirmed facts of which I was unsure. They are for me quintessential ranchers, the spirit of these hills. There are many families around Ericson like them—ranch families tied to the land for generations, people who continue to define these hills, even as they become depopulated, even as the practice of family ranching fades: the Patricks, Dahlstens, Vechs, Kasselders, Bodyfields, Ericksons, Brinkmans, Pitzers, Losekes, Pelsters, Buckles, Renners, Hoefners, Bumgardners, and Olsons.

Besides her ranch responsibilities, Carol Olson fills the role of postmaster in Ericson, a job she also held in 1984, when I would drive daily to town and stop at the post office. Carol, with her snappy blue eyes and friendly demeanor, always drew me into a conversation. We often talked of books, sharing the titles of our favorites, discussing ideas and the fate of humankind. Outside the postmaster's window hung notices of anniversary parties and wedding dances, and thank-you notes for kindnesses extended to ailing community members. The post office still serves as the clearinghouse for community news, and Carol always knows the latest about people who are recuperating in hospitals in Grand Island, Lincoln, or Omaha.

I haven't seen Dixie Foster in years, and I understand Laura Gordon has moved to Lincoln. Derald Watson is gone, and my cousin Miles lives in California. Some have stayed, though. An old friend, Frank Wietzki, runs the Hungry Horse and does a good business, too. His prime rib nights draw people from all over the hills. He's invented some special sauce he puts on the meat—made up the recipe himself, but won't tell it to a soul—and news of the Hungry Horse Saloon and prime rib dinners has spread throughout the state.

Clarence and Wilma, who ran the Hungry Horse when I was in Ericson in 1984, sold out some years ago. They planned to retire in Ericson, but Clarence died suddenly. Wilma still lives in town.

Since 1984 a few more businesses have closed. Spilinek's Hardware was one. Bob just couldn't make a go of it. "I stay open for the locals," he told me once, but that was not enough to sustain the business. He closed the store several years ago and went to work for Foxley's. Foster's Market closed up, too. Mike and Blanche had run the store since long before my time. As they grew older their son stepped in to help, but there wasn't enough trade to keep two grocery stores going in town. Now only Pat's Market sells the staples that locals need. Most people travel to Ord, Burwell, or Grand Island to stock up on food and household supplies. The service station and bank are still in operation, and the Salebarn north of town has been taken over by new people who seem to be doing a good job at bringing back the business. The Salebarn's Ranch Café serves breakfast and lunch most days.

North and west of town the Pitzer Ranch continues to carry on its horse business, drawing people from around the country who want to breed horses or buy Pitzer stock. In 1993, when my husband

and I were passing through, we took a drive in the prairie around Ericson one day. Each of us carried a thirty-five-millimeter camera. We were planning to capture images of the landscape when the fire whistle blew. We swung by the volunteer fire department to find out where the problem was.

"Out at Pitzer's," somebody called, jumping into the cab of one of the pump trucks. "Prairie fire!" We followed the line of trucks and fire engines dashing north out of town and up the River Road toward the Pitzer Ranch, turned in at a pasture gate, and rumbled across prairie. Ahead, flames lapped at a wooded area, spreading into downed and dried cottonwood trees. Over a hill, smoke rose. It was a contagious moment; we couldn't help what happened next. We parked my father's pickup and climbed out to make some photographs. Everything around us was action, though—trucks and pickups racing by, volunteers spraying water, wind chasing voices— and it was clear they needed all the help they could get.

Gene, my husband, said, "I'm going to jump on the next truck that comes by," and he didn't have to wait long. A pump truck sailed in our direction. "You need help?" Gene called out. An arm reached down; he reached up. In seconds he was in the truck, waving as they sped up a prairie dune. I hoofed it over the next rise. Another truck barreled in my direction. "Can I help?" I called.

"Get in." A door swung open, and I leaped in with two men. We crested the hill, and before us fingers of flame, whipped by wind, burned across grass, moving fast, consuming this dry prairie. The pickup stopped; the men leaped out. "Here, take a shovel." A man thrust one into my hand. "Stay behind the flames," he called, running down the hill toward the nearest front of fire, and I ran too, hefting my shovel, following him into the smoke.

People chased the flames across prairie, beating at them with old rugs, smothering them with dirt. Pump trucks crawled over the hills, spraying water. I watched others with shovels and learned quickly how to shovel, toss, and run at the same time, keeping pace with the line of flame. Smoke filled the air. At times I could hardly breathe, but everyone kept running up and down hills, so I ran, too.

I can't say how long we fought the blaze, but finally it was under control; the pump trucks followed up earlier foot assaults, dowsing land with water. I made my way back to the pickup, covered with soot and smelling of fire. Several men were standing around, leaning on shovels. I pulled my camera from the cab of the truck and caught them in a couple of images; then we piled into the pickup and drove the edges of the burned area, working our way out of the field, stopping every time we saw a smoldering cow chip. "They hold the fire and can restart a blaze later," one cowboy told me. He jumped out and broke up each smoking chip. When the men dropped me off at my dad's pickup, Gene was there, covered in grime, too, and smelling of smoke. We climbed into the Dodge and drove to the Hungry Horse for a beer. Back at the Big Six, my father did not seem surprised that we would turn up covered with dirt and ash and smelling of smoke. It seemed perfectly natural to him that we would dash off into the hills to fight a fire with these people of Ericson, in a place I call home.

The next day Gene and I drove back to the burned prairie to see the damage a fire like that can do. Blackened trails rolled across the hills, edged by brown unburned grass, marking the limits of the fire. We took several pictures, wandering through the burn, following sandy tracks up and down dunes, inspecting cacti that had survived and still bloomed. Behind us a big truck crested a dune and rolled down to where we stood. Inside were Howard Pitzer and his wife, Florence. We were trespassing, of course, and I figured we were in for it. We talked for several minutes, explaining who we were, that we had fought the fire the day before, that we were curious about the land and had come back to make some photographs.

"Take all the pictures you want," he called as he turned the truck around and headed home. "I'd sure like to see some of those when they're done."

It was on that same journey in 1993 that I saw a man who used to frequent the Someplace Else. He was a boy then, who spooked like a wild pony; he was the one who used to come in and gaze at me late on summer weekend nights. I saw him at the Salebarn in

Ericson with his wife and child. He saw me, too, and looked away quickly, never to look my way again.

I've never been back to the Someplace Else. I heard that Jack and Eve split up and sold the bar. It wouldn't be the same now, so I avoid the place and the regulars I came to know. Once though—I think it was in 1992, about a year before Gene and I left Iowa for Oregon—I was traveling through the hills, returning from a conference in Kearney. I stayed in a motel in Loup City, and I don't know what possessed me. It was late at night and wind howled around the corners of the building. Fall was almost over and winter was coming into the land. I reached beneath the motel desktop, pulled open the drawer, lifted out the phone book, and thumbed to the page for numbers in the little town where Parker's parents had lived. I'm not sure what I was looking for, but I found what I suppose I needed to find. There in the listings under Parker's last name was a number for Parker—and a woman: "Hastings," it said, "Parker and Kate." I gazed at the page for a long time, playing back that summer, wind racing through the eaves of that outback motel. Then I closed the book, returned it to the drawer, and got on with my life, driving east in the morning, back to Augustana College and my teaching job.

As for the future of water in the hills, little has changed. The aquifer is still pumped all over the Great Plains to water crops. In Nebraska alone the number of registered wells increased from 70,233 in 1984 to 76,363 in 1994, and cattle and corn continue to dominate agriculture in the state. In 1992 cash receipts for cattle and corn in Nebraska totaled over six and a half billion dollars, making up nearly seventy-five percent of the state's agricultural income.

During the 1980s there was some experimentation with processes to address losses to the aquifer. One plan explored the feasibility of recharging the aquifer with river water, but that was a confused solution, the kind that just goes in circles: Borrow water from one place and put it in another.

In the early 1990s there was talk of funneling federal money into projects that would reverse the decline in the Ogallala Aquifer, but a few years of good rain have diminished interest in those projects. "Rainfall levels have been good the last couple of years," a congressional aide in Lincoln mused recently in a phone conversation, "and the Nebraska portion of the aquifer has been recharged, so no one is interested in legislation about the aquifer now." But in the dry years, he indicated, there would be renewed concern for the water of the aquifer.

In the meantime, Nebraska has created "natural resource districts" that manage each region of the state and have the authority to institute control areas where the quantity of water pumped is regulated. To date, two such districts have utilized that authority. Kansas has similar resource districts, but Texas has only a voluntary program. To say that a unified and aggressive strategy to address overuse of the aquifer has been developed would be an exaggeration. No one wants to say the bogey word: "corn." No one wants to say that what needs to happen in Nebraska is that less corn be grown and irrigated with water from the Ogallala Aquifer. No one wants to suggest a return to dry-land farming and a shift to crops that do not require the kind of moisture that corn requires. No one wants to face the fact that the day will come when the water just won't be there. Scientists predict that at the current rate of extraction, irrigation on the Great Plains could last about another fifty to a hundred years.

Several weeks ago my husband told me a story about a friend of ours back in Iowa. He'd bought a cabin at a lake in northwest Iowa that had been a haven for him during his childhood, and now his children were going there during summers and vacations. "Their lives will be forever different," he said, "because they have that place in their childhood."

I realized that I, too, have been irrevocably changed by Ericson and the Big Six Country Club. I would have been a different kind of little girl, I would have grown into a different kind of woman, if I had had only Osceola, Nebraska, in my childhood life. But because I had Ericson, because I had the Sandhills, I am changed; I am a woman today with a voice shaped by an early life spent in the natural world. I am changed because of Ericson, and because of Ericson, I cannot be silent about the things I love.

September 1995
Oregon

$\mathscr{A}$CKNOWLEDGMENTS

I wish to thank my father, Judge William Hayden Norton; my mother, Nancy Sayre Somermeyer; and my brother, William Hayden Norton, Jr., for helping me remember the details, for clarifying facts, and for understanding that I had to tell this story. I want to recognize my grandmother Catherine Hayden Norton, who still lives in Osceola, and my grandfather William Wendell Norton, who died twenty-seven years ago, as the people who initiated our family involvement with the Sandhills. Bless you for this gift.

Many people in Nebraska helped as I created this book. Special thanks go to Dick and Bonnadel Foster, Carol Olson, Frank Wietzki, and Bob and Teddi Spilinek. Alice Dentler offered friendship and a wealth of information, and the following individuals helped gather and confirm facts: Jim Barr in Congressman Doug Bereuter's office, Robert Kuzelka at the University of Nebraska Water Center, Nancy Thramer at the Agricultural Stabilization and Conservation Service office in Burwell, and Lin Hagen at the University of Nebraska C. Y. Thompson Library.

My deepest gratitude goes to Georganne O'Connor—fine writer and friend—who gave constant support during the process of this book.

Thanks also travel on wings to Terry Tempest Williams, who

believed in me and repeatedly offered just the right words at just the right time.

I wish to acknowledge my writing friends around the country—Liz Carpenter, Barbara Stahura, Julene Bair, and Sharon Russell—whose wisdom, friendship, and knowledge have comforted and guided.

Kathy Hanson believed in me for all the years during which I moved back and forth across the country. Her friendship shines like a beacon in the night.

In the Nehalem Bay area of Oregon, where I live now, many folks listened and offered encouragement: Mark Nelson, Norma Seely, Greg Movsesyan, Don Osborne, and Alisa Carlson. Thank you.

I owe a special debt of gratitude to Esther Bell, massage therapist extraordinaire, who kept my arms working when there was no good reason that they should.

I wish to acknowledge the John F. Murray Fund at the University of Iowa School of Journalism and Mass Communications for a grant that helped me start this book, and John Bennett, my adviser when I was a student in that program, who offered friendship, advice, and guidance, and who was perhaps the first to evoke in me the possibility of writing a book. Also, I want to thank the Faculty Research Committee of Augustana College in Rock Island, Illinois, for a generous grant that helped make this book a reality, and my former colleagues and friends in the English department who believed in me tirelessly, even when I chose to leave that institution for a different kind of life. I specifically want to mention Karin Youngberg, Roald Tweet, Don Erickson, Nancy Huse, and Joan Robinson.

My agent, Elizabeth Backman, deserves a roomful of tulips for her dedication and persistence, and I thank my editor, George Witte, for his insight and careful shepherding of this story.

My feline companion, Ms. Brit, who brought me great joy each day I wrote, died in December 1995. I simply want to acknowledge the great gift that animals can give.

In the end, I must thank Gene, who has helped me build this

writing life, who has traveled with me on my journeys—both interior and exterior—who shares my love of landscape, who offered
advice, shaped this book, read multiple drafts, and, through the
years, has been my most ardent supporter. He is the safe port from
which I journey forth.